# PRAISE FOR *WITNESS AT THE CROSS*

In each chapter of *Witness at the Cross*, Levine parses out the Gospel's witness accounts of Jesus's crucifixion and invites readers to be transformed by this theological symphony of the cross. This informative, witty, and accessible study provides a welcome preaching and teaching resource for clergy and laity. Small group leaders will also appreciate its six-chapter format ideal for a Lenten study.

—**Rev. Dr. Deborah Appler**, Professor of Hebrew Bible,
Moravian Theological Seminary

Amy-Jill Levine reminds us that the story of Jesus's death is something we do not just read; we are meant to experience it. In *Witness at the Cross*, she takes us by the hand and walks with us through the story, pausing alongside each of the characters to see and hear and feel how they individually experienced it, how each was affected by it. This is not just a fresh retelling of the Crucifixion narrative; it is a remarkably personal immersion and participation in the narrative. Amy-Jill Levine breaks open new dimensions and possibilities of the story's meaning for all of us.

—**Larry J. Beasley**, Presbytery Leader and Stated Clerk,
Presbytery of Utica

This is a timely and important introduction to the events of Holy Friday. Levine's approach is scholarly yet personal, theologically sophisticated yet devotional. She does a masterful job sorting through the perspectives of the Gospel writers, showing readers what each evangelist accentuates and the things each writer wants us to think more deeply about and to question when it comes to our own experience of the world today. This is the best possible resource for either reflective reading or a study group.

—**Rev. Dr. John S. McClure**, Charles G. Finney
Professor of Preaching and Worship, Emeritus,
Vanderbilt Divinity School

Witness at the Cross

# Witness at the Cross
# A Beginner's Guide to Holy Friday

### Witness at the Cross
978-1-7910-2112-2
978-1-7910-2113-9 *eBook*

### Witness at the Cross DVD
978-1-7910-2122-1

### Witness at the Cross Leader Guide
978-1-7910-2114-6
978-1-7910-2115-3 *eBook*

---

## Also by Amy-Jill Levine

*Entering the Passion of Jesus*
*A Beginner's Guide to Holy Week*

*Light of the World*
*A Beginner's Guide to Advent*

*Sermon on the Mount*
*A Beginner's Guide to the Kingdom of Heaven*

*The Difficult Words of Jesus*
*A Beginner's Guide to His Most Perplexing Teachings*

# AMY-JILL LEVINE

# WITNESS
## *at the* CROSS

### A BEGINNER'S GUIDE *to* HOLY FRIDAY

Abingdon Press | Nashville

## Witness at the Cross
## A Beginner's Guide to Holy Friday

**Library of Congress Control Number: 2021946826**
978-1-7910-2112-2

21 22 23 24 25 26 27 28 29 30 — 10 9 8 7 6 5 4 3 2 1
MANUFACTURED IN THE UNITED STATES OF AMERICA

*For Elizabeth Caldwell
and Ann Neely*

# CONTENTS

# Introduction

## SIMON OF CYRENE

Gospel evidence does not provide a precise setting for the Crucifixion. Matthew 27:33, Mark 15:22, and John 19:17 call it Golgotha, an Aramaic term meaning "[place of] the Skull"; the Greek word is *kranion* (whence "cranium"). Luke, who tends to avoid Aramaic, calls it "The Skull" (Luke 23:33). The Latin gives us "Calvary." Artists tend to depict the site as a hill—and so presume that the cross could be seen from afar—and the name could come from a cranium-shaped plot of land; it could also come from the bones of other victims, unceremoniously tossed into a pit on the site. The Gospel of John 19:20 suggests it was "near the city," meaning Jerusalem. From the time of Helena, the mother of Constantine the emperor, the site has been identified as near the Church of the Holy Sepulchre.

That Jesus was crucified I have no doubt. That we do not know the exact location should be a prompt for reflection rather than consternation. Such speculation begins as early as the New Testament itself. The Epistle to the Hebrews 13:12 understands the location theologically: "Therefore Jesus also suffered outside the city gate in order to sanctify the people by his own blood." For this author, "outside the city gate" fits the view that the followers of Jesus are spiritually not at home in the Roman Empire where their movement is more often denounced than embraced. Speaking not of the Jerusalem Temple but of the sanctuary around which the Exodus generation lived in the wilderness, between Egyptian slavery and return to the Promised Land, the author urges, "Let us then go to him outside the camp and bear the abuse he endured. For here we have no lasting city, but we are looking for a city that is to come" (Hebrews 13:13-14).

The "Skull" suggests mortality, but at the same it reminds us that Jesus gave his life as a ransom for many (Matthew 20:28; Mark 10:45). Good Friday anticipates Easter; death anticipates resurrection. Perhaps we are reminded of the cranium, the part of our anatomy that encloses the brain and that is related to our sensory organs. This notice suggests that the story of Jesus's death is something that we do not just read: we think about it, and we experience it; we hear the taunts of the soldiers, the priests, and the passersby even as we hear the famous "seven last words" (there are actually more) from the cross. We taste the gall held up to Jesus's lips even as we feel his thirst. We inhale the fetid smells of sweat, of blood, and of death, and then the hundred pounds of spice Nicodemus and Joseph of Arimathea use to provide Jesus's body a royal entombment. We touch each other, as did the Beloved Disciple when he took the mother of Jesus to his home. We feel the wind blowing in the darkness, and we sense the Holy Spirit. With the tearing of the Temple curtain, we recognize that the universe is in mourning.

We filter these visions through the witnesses at the cross. Each saw something different. Each needed something from Jesus, and in turn, he needed them as well, for that is what it means to so love the world (John 3:16). Rabbi Abraham Joshua Heschel's book, *God in Search of Man*, shows how the God of Israel wants to be in relationship with all of humanity, and so does Jesus. The Jewish and Christian traditions tell us that God needs us. It is through our hands and feet, our mouths that speak and our hearts and minds that prompt us to act, that God's work is seen in the world.

Each Evangelist presents a distinct picture of the death of Jesus. Each portrays different individuals and groups of people at the cross, each offers different images and dialogues, and so each leaves a different theological message. Yet they work together to create a theological symphony. Each Gospel narrative is only partial; each invites interpretation; all invite readers to use our senses to interpret anew stories that are told and retold. The more I read the accounts of these witnesses, the more I see connections to the Scriptures of Israel, to earlier material in each Gospel, and to the messages that the Gospels offer their readers.

The witnesses at the cross are numerous. The Gospels of Matthew, Mark, and Luke, called "Synoptic" because they "see" [optic] "together" ["syn," as in synthesis or synagogue], have the same basic story. They present bystanders, including priests, scribes, and elders, whom we meet in chapter 1. Some of the bystanders blaspheme (that is the Greek term used; most English translations offer "deride," which is a good translation) Jesus: "Aha! You who would destroy the temple and build it in three days, save yourself, and come down from the cross!" (Mark 15:29-30). Their words prompt attention to what Jesus did say about the Temple, the role of false testimony, and how Jesus's followers came to understand him as the new temple. When they facetiously call out, "If you are the Son of God, come down from the cross" (Matthew 27:40b), they place themselves in the role of Satan, who similarly tempted Jesus to prove his status by serving himself.

The chief priests taunt Jesus to save himself as he saved others. Ironically, they witness that Jesus did save, and so they open for us discussion of what salvation did, and can, mean. The term *save* can connote "rescue" or even "heal"; so the salvation offered by the cross cannot be separated from the attention to ailing bodies and spirits. More, we'll see how by dying, Jesus is engaging in another act of salvation, for as he had noted, those who want to save their lives must lose them (Matthew 16:25; Mark 8:35; Luke 9:24). Jesus never asks of others what he would not do himself.

According to the Gospels of Matthew and Mark, some of the bystanders think Jesus is calling Elijah. They are incorrect: Jesus is not calling Elijah; he is rather citing the first verse of Psalm 22: "My God, my God, why have you forsaken me?" As we shall see throughout the study, the psalm—which you might want to read now—underlines the narrative: the taunting, the casting of lots for the garments, the thirst, the other doers of evil. The ending of the psalm, which Jesus does not speak, also influences how we understand his cry, for the psalm ends with the universal praise of God. Indeed, psalms were meant to be prayed by anyone, and thus any reader can pray the same psalm Jesus prays, with the same faith he had.

Chapter 2 introduces the two men crucified with Jesus, one on his right hand and one on his left. According to the Gospels of Mark and Matthew, these two men taunt Jesus as do the chief priests, soldiers, and other bystanders; the one thing to which all these disparate constituencies can agree is that they hate someone else, an ancient example of scapegoating. Only in Luke's Gospel does Jesus finally receive some sympathy from others. Here the so-called "good thief" joins the chorus of Pilate, Herod Antipas, and the centurion at the cross in proclaiming Jesus righteous and thus innocent of the crime of sedition for which he is sentenced. Of all the witnesses at the cross, only he acknowledges that Jesus rules a kingdom, and only to this penitent does Jesus promise, "Today you will be with me in Paradise" (Luke 23:43).

The chapter turns us to people convicted, incarcerated, and executed of crimes today, as well as to the often-difficult task of sorting among the charges, for one person's terrorist is another person's freedom fighter. We also hear the desperation of the other victim, who cries out, "Are you not the Messiah? Save yourself and us!" (Luke 23:39b). For a bystander to taunt Jesus is cruel; for someone dying at the same time, with the same pain, the taunt is desperation. This second victim does not recognize that in dying, Jesus is offering his life as salvation.

The penitent victim tells Jesus to "remember" him, and so opens the topic of memory: who will remember us, and whom will we remember? More, will we be remembered, and what will be the last words we speak or hear, or what we want to say and hear?

In chapter 3 we meet the soldiers: the men who cast lots for Jesus's clothes (victims of crucifixion were stripped before being affixed to the cross, and thus humiliation is added to the torture), and the centurion who announces, astoundingly in Mark and Matthew's Gospels, that Jesus was "a son of God." Luke rephrases the centurion's comment to "Surely this man was righteous" (most English translations read "innocent"—and I'll be fussing at translations all the way through). The presence of the soldiers raises questions not only about military operations and colonial rule but also about Christology: why, for example, does an anonymous centurion correctly identify Jesus when, at least in Mark's account, his own disciples have deserted him?

The centurion also raises matters of conscience. Can we see him as "just following orders" when he executes a man he deems righteous if not divine? Is "just following orders" ever a good explanation? What do we do if we convict someone, not just in a judicial setting but also in a judgmental comment or a piece of gossip, and then realize that we have made a dreadful mistake?

Chapter 4 introduces the Beloved Disciple or the "Disciple Whom Jesus Loved"—like the centurion at the cross, the Beloved Disciple comes to us anonymously in the Fourth Gospel, although tradition identifies him as John, the son of Zebedee (we'll meet Mrs. Zebedee in chapter 5—I really like Mrs. Zebedee), the purported author of the Gospel. Only John's Gospel depicts this disciple, and only in John's Gospel does a disciple stand not at a distance but close to the cross. Only in the Fourth Gospel as well do we have the Beloved Disciple resting on Jesus's breast at the Last Supper. This anonymous follower reappears at the tomb and then in the last scene of the Gospel, at the breakfast by the lake. Real, composite, or a bit of both, the Beloved Disciple is the authority behind the Fourth Gospel, but he can also be any of us, at any time, standing at the cross, *being noticed*, and then *being commissioned.*

Jesus entrusts his mother—never identified as Mary in the Fourth Gospel—to the Disciple's care and thereby sets up a new family unit, or what today we call a blended family. We can see the Disciple and the mother as enacting Jesus's mandate: "I give you a new commandment, that you love one another. Just as I have loved you, you also should love on another" (John 13:34). The Beloved Disciple will now care for an older woman. Anyone who has engaged in such care knows the commitment and the sacrifices involved.

In chapter 5 we meet Jesus's mother and the other women at the cross, whether watching at a distance (so the Synoptics) or standing close by (so the Fourth Gospel). Mark tells us, in chapter 15 of 16, after describing the death of Jesus, that women from the Galilee had been with the mission the entire time—a bit late, Mark. Matthew makes special mention of Zebedee's wife, the original helicopter parent (did I mention that I like her?), who appears at the cross but not at the tomb. Luke introduces both the "daughters of Jerusalem" who weep for Jesus and the patrons of the movement who support Jesus financially. John places the mother of Jesus at the cross—and depending on how we understand the identification of the other women, so might the Synoptics.

In Mark's Gospel, the three named women at the cross are also the witnesses to the tomb, and it is they who on Easter morning seek to anoint the body. Yet, in Mark's Gospel, the body has already been anointed for its burial earlier in the week. We can see these three named women, "Mary Magdalene, and Mary the mother of James the younger and of Joses, and Salome" (Mark 15:40), in parallel to the three named men at Gethsemane, Peter, James, and John. Each trio is well intended, but at the Gospel's abrupt end in Mark 16:8, each trio fails. And yet we know, the empty tomb is not the end of the story. In Matthew's Gospel, the women do not go to anoint but to watch, and their fidelity is rewarded by Jesus's first resurrection appearance. Luke gives us numerous women who witness the empty tomb and experience an angelophany (a good word for the day), but the male disciples refuse to believe their story. The concern here is not that Jewish men rejected the idea of women as credible witnesses (a comment I've often heard); the concern is the witness itself, since the disciples could not imagine that Jesus would be raised from the dead.

Finally, we turn to Joseph of Arimathea and Nicodemus. Usually associated with Jesus's entombment, they are also the ones responsible for the deposition, the technical term for the removal of the body from the cross (I like this term because it is also used in the legal sense regarding taking testimony from witnesses). We'll see how Joseph morphs from a member of the Sanhedrin who votes to convict Jesus to a secret disciple and how Nicodemus, who never quite shows conviction that Jesus is Lord, reveals himself as a friend and ally, like many people in the pews today.

The conclusion adduces a few other witnesses to the cross—nature, from the darkness at noon to earthquakes, and then God, present to receive the spirit of Jesus, and mourning as symbolized by the rending of the Temple veil. Throughout, we'll find allusions to other witnesses, from prophecy in earlier texts to reception history, the study of how these various stories were interpreted over time.

We travel through these stories with our first witness, Simon of Cyrene, another figure who enters and exits the text, leaving only tantalizing clues as to who he is and what he might have to say to us.

## Simon of Cyrene

Mark's Gospel, likely the earliest of the four, tells us that after Pilate had Jesus flogged, the Roman soldiers mocked Jesus, crowned him with thorns, and then "led him out to crucify him" (Mark 15:20). The upright poles of the crosses were already planted; the victims would be compelled to carry the crossbeam. Although the Gospel does not dwell on the point, Jesus is probably too weak to bear the weight. When Mark 15:22 states that they "brought" Jesus to the cross—the Greek term conveys the sense of "bear" or "carry"—we can imagine that they dragged him those last steps. For Mark, the crucified Christ fully empties himself, "taking the form of a slave," since crucifixion was the punishment for slaves and enemies of the state, and "humbles himself to death" (I am alluding to the Christ Hymn in Philippians 2:6-11).

The Evangelist then reports that these soldiers "compelled a passer-by, who was coming in from the country, to carry his cross: it was Simon of Cyrene, the father of Alexander and Rufus" (Mark 15:21). While so many characters in Mark's Gospel, including all the other people at the cross, save for the women looking on from a distance, are nameless, Mark records this fellow's name, what he had been doing, his place of birth, and his children. And then, nothing. In one verse Simon enters and then vanishes from the text. Why these details? Why nothing more? The detail Mark gives prompts speculation, interpretation, and sometimes revision as the other Gospels offer their own stories of how Jesus made his way to the cross.

Matthew 27:32 simply notes that the soldiers "came upon a man from Cyrene named Simon; they compelled this man to carry his cross." Luke 23:26 makes the soldiers' action more visceral: "They seized a man, Simon of Cyrene, who was coming in from the country, and they laid the cross on him, and made him carry it behind Jesus."

The Fourth Gospel, for reasons both practical and theological, omits any mention of Simon of Cyrene. John 19:17 insists that Jesus was "carrying the cross by himself." The Johannine Jesus is not weakened; he is fully in control of body, mind, and spirit. More, John's account functions to squash rumors that had begun to flourish that it was not Jesus but Simon of Cyrene who had been crucified; still others thought that when Jesus said, "My God, my God, why have you forsaken me?" (Mark 15:34), he was speaking of the Holy Spirit fleeing from the cross. Stories always give rise to other stories, and sometimes those new stories wander into the realm of what would later be considered heresy.

My introduction to Simon of Cyrene, apart from a few stylized "stations of the cross" (#5 or #7, depending on the system of counting), was, as best as I can remember, George Stevens's classic *The Greatest Story Ever Told*. Sidney Poitier—whom I knew from *To Sir, with Love*, *In the Heat of the Night*, and *Guess Who's Coming to Dinner*, portrays Simon of Cyrene. We do not know if the original Simon of Cyrene was Jewish (I suspect he was; there was a very large Jewish community in Cyrene at the time), but I think he was, given that no Gentile mission had yet begun. Simon of Cyrene was likely a Black Jew, one of countless others.

Cyrene is in North Africa (present-day Libya), and Simon reminds me also of the Jewish Diaspora. In case you're not sure where Libya is, you will have likely heard of several of its cities, including Tripoli, Tobruk, and, more recently, Benghazi. During the Second World War, Libya, then ruled by Italy, first set up laws restricting the rights of Jews; then the deportation of the Jewish population by the Germans began. Those Jews who remained, or lived through the war to return, faced the same violence as did other Jews in majority Muslim nations at the founding of the state of Israel in 1948. In the next three years, because of this violence coupled with ongoing legal discrimination, three-quarters of Libya's Jewish population (more than thirty thousand people) emigrated. After the Six Day War (between Israel and the combined forces of the United Arab Republic [Egypt], Syria, and Jordan) in June 1967, the Italian navy helped evacuate six thousand Libyan Jews to Italy, so by the time Colonel Muammar Gaddafi took power (1969-2011), only about a hundred Jews remained. The last Jew to live in Libya left in 2000. Simon of Cyrene, ironically, becomes the prompt to remember communities that no longer exist because of ethnic cleansing.

Simon may have relocated his family to Judea to be closer to Jerusalem; perhaps he had relatives there; perhaps he expected the kingdom of God to be centered in a Jerusalem liberated from the Romans. That Mark knows the names of his two sons gives the impression that Alexander and Rufus were members of the community gathered in Jesus's name or at least well known to them.

I wonder what Simon told his sons. Did he realize whose cross he was carrying: a criminal or a king? Had he heard Jesus's comment, "If anyone forces you to go one mile, go also the second" (Matthew 5:41)? The connection here is the word *compel* in Greek, which is the same word Matthew 27:32 and Mark 15:21 use to describe how the soldiers "compelled" Simon to carry the crossbeam. I can also picture Alexander and Rufus, at the retelling of the Passion narrative, insisting on the reference to their father, if not to themselves as well: "Remember to state that he was coming in from the fields...remember to say that he was from Cyrene [cheers from Cyreneans can be heard in the background], remember to note that he was compelled..." Perhaps this is the same Rufus whom Paul mentions in Romans

16:13: "Greet Rufus, chosen in the Lord; and greet his mother—a mother to me also." Perhaps the two sons were among the "men of Cyprus and Cyrene" who, scattered from Jerusalem following Stephen's execution according to Luke in Acts 11:19-20, began to evangelize in Antioch. Were they remembered because they had an important father, or did they make their own mark?

Simon can be seen as epitomizing the victim of the police state. Minding his own business, he is compelled to carry someone else's cross. On the other hand, he is anyone who, whether voluntarily or not, bears someone else's burden. Luke states that he walks behind Jesus, and thus Simon models the disciple, for as Jesus says, "If any want to become my followers, let them deny themselves and take up their cross daily and follow me" (Luke 9:23; see also Matthew 10:38; 16:24; Mark 8:34; Luke 14:27).

We might picture Simon at the cross, perhaps giving Jesus words of comfort as his wrists and ankles are nailed to the wood. Perhaps the soldiers swatted him away; perhaps he joined the women at a distance. Perhaps his sons were with him, and they, too, saw the supporters, the sympathizers, the busybodies, the scoffers, the soldiers, the women, the Beloved Disciple, and the mother of Jesus.

Each Gospel has its own story to tell, all the witnesses have their own memories, and every reader comes away with a new insight. The witnesses at the Crucifixion watch Jesus die, and we watch with them, and we watch them. And we come away transformed.

# Chapter 1

# BYSTANDERS AND SCOFFERS

Golgotha is heavily populated: Simon of Cyrene; the two men executed together with Jesus; the women, including Mary Magdalene and the mother of Jesus, whether at a distance or by the foot of the cross; the centurion and other soldiers; Joseph of Arimathea and Nicodemus; the Beloved Disciple. And there are the others: the chief priests and scribes who mock Jesus, and the bystanders who hear his words and witness the natural events marking his death. We turn first to the chief priests and their affiliates, whose historical presence at the cross I doubt, but whose literary message speaks volumes. Then we look at the bystanders in the Gospels of Matthew and Mark who deride Jesus for making statements against the Temple and think Jesus is calling Elijah. In all four accounts, someone offers Jesus a sponge soaked with sour wine, but the meaning of the gesture changes.

The Gospels are extraordinarily sparse in detailing Jesus's crucifixion—the nails, the pain—they instead focus on the responses and reactions of Jesus and the witnesses. They therefore pose questions: about our desire to deride others and to gloat at their misfortunes, about what we expect from Jesus as Lord and Savior, about how we interpret what we hear. They ask us about bystanders—are there any innocent bystanders? When we heard of children being separated at the border, what did we do? If we are against capital punishment, do we try to stop the execution? Are lighting candles outside and praying enough? What do we do when we know something, sponsored by the state, or by the religious group to which we belong, is wrong?

They ask us, in the words of the old spiritual, "Were you there when they crucified my Lord?" and then they do more by asking, "What would you have thought, or done, had you been there?"

Nobody said this was going to be easy. As always, getting to Easter means time at the cross and time at the tomb.

## The Different Perspectives

The passersby play different roles in the Gospels, as we might expect, since each Evangelist has different points to make. For Mark and Matthew, they are part of the chorus that taunts Jesus, along with the chief priests, elders, scribes, and soldiers, and the other victims being crucified. In Luke's account, the "people stood by, watching," while "the leaders scoffed" at Jesus (Luke 23:35). To what extent do the leaders speak for the people, and to what extent should they be differentiated? The question is more difficult today, in a participatory democracy wherein leaders are elected, than in antiquity, where the chief priests hold office both because of genealogy (they are of priestly descent, traced back to Moses's brother, Aaron) and because Rome recognizes their legal authority in Judea. It was Pontius Pilate, the Roman governor, who maintained Caiaphas in the role of high priest.

For Matthew and Mark, Jesus dies with the cry, "My God, my God, why have you forsaken me?" a cry that reflects also the unity of enmity surrounding him. Luke's Jesus does not die with an Aramaic prayer; Luke tends to avoid Aramaic (we've seen with Luke's "the place that is called the Skull" rather than "Golgotha"). Nor does Jesus die deserted or in despair. While he is ridiculed (the Greek has a sense of turning up one's nose) by priests and elders, the soldiers, and one of the other two victims, he is also supported. The people here "watch" (Luke 23:35) rather than sneer; among them are the daughters of Jerusalem who wept for him. Further, in Luke's account Jesus receives support not only from the so-called "good thief" or "penitent thief" but also by the palpable presence of the divine. Now Jesus dies with the address "Father" and then a citation from Psalm 31:5, "Into your hand I commit my spirit." The next line of the psalm is "You have redeemed me, O LORD, faithful God."

The Fourth Gospel depicts no chief priests, scribes, or elders at the cross. This depiction may be more historically accurate, as it would be odd for the chief priests, who work in the Temple and therefore should maintain states of ritual purity, to be at the site of executions and so in proximity to dead bodies. While burying a corpse is a major religious act in Judaism—it's one of the few acts we perform on behalf of others for which there is no possibility of reciprocation, since the corpse cannot do anything for us—it does make one ritually impure. On the other hand, these priests would not be the first or the last representatives of a religious institution to be guilty of hypocrisy.

In John's Gospel, there are no mocking passersby. The Fourth Gospel depicts Jesus as so fully in control that he chooses to take a sip of the wine offered to him and then announces, "It is finished" (John 19:30). The NRSV here reads, "Then he bowed his head and gave up his spirit": the King James Version offers the famous "[He] gave up the ghost."

## The Passersby

According to Mark 15:29-30a, "Those who passed by derided him, shaking their heads and saying, 'Aha! You who would destroy the temple and build it in three days, save yourself and come down from the cross!'" Their headshaking possibly alludes to Psalm

22:7, "All who see me mock at me; they make mouths at me, / they shake their heads." The term the NRSV renders "derided" is the Greek term "to blaspheme." While the term primarily means to "abuse verbally," the connotation of blasphemy, an offense against God, is not inappropriate. For Mark, to abuse Jesus is to abuse God. The irony: at the Sanhedrin trial, Caiaphas condemns Jesus for blasphemy (it's a trumped-up charge, for Jesus did not blaspheme), when the passersby are the ones who literally blaspheme. The reference to the Temple reminds us of Jesus's action there, and it also reminds us of the "false witnesses" who, at the Sanhedrin trial, accused Jesus of speaking against the Temple.

Following the darkness from noon to three o'clock, Jesus cries out in Aramaic, "Eloi, Eloi, lema sabachthani?" which Mark translates into Greek as, "My God, my God, why have you forsaken me?" (Mark 15:34). The bystanders think that Jesus is calling for Elijah, since *Eloi* (or, closer, Matthew's *Eli*) sounds like the ancient prophet's name. Mark then recounts, "someone ran, filled a sponge with sour wine, put it on a stick, and gave it to him to drink, saying, 'Wait, let us see whether Elijah will come to take him down'" (Mark 15:36).

Mark has, in a few short verses, introduced numerous themes established in the Gospel: Jesus's relationship to the Temple, the cry of dereliction from Psalm 22, the concern for Elijah, and several other fulfillment citations. In all these instances, Mark positions us readers in a privileged role: we know more than the bystanders. We understand that Jesus does not remain abandoned, for we know the end of the story. Jesus had predicted both his abandonment and the restitution of relationship: he tells his disciples, "You will all become deserters; for it is written, / 'I will strike the shepherd, / and the sheep will be scattered' [Zechariah 13:7]. / But after I am raised up, I will go before you to Galilee" (Mark 14:27-28). Since the scattering has come true, the reappearance will come true as well. And we also understand that Jesus is *not* calling Elijah, for since we know the rest of the Gospel of Mark, we know that Elijah has already come twice: once as the Baptizer and second at the Transfiguration.

## The Temple

The passersby taunt Jesus, "You who would destroy the temple and build it in three days…" (Mark 15:29). We might have thought this accusation would come from the chief priests, who oversaw the Temple's activities. Instead, distinct charges hint at distinct issues. The chief priests focus on the political, the "king of Israel," since they are the nominal rulers. No need for a king, they may be thinking, since we have governmental authority. Jesus died sometime between 26 and 36 CE, the years Pontius Pilate was the Roman-appointed governor. There will be a king of Judea in 41 to 44, when Rome proclaimed the rule of Agrippa I, the grandson of Herod the Great. Agrippa I appears in Acts 12:1-2, where he kills James the brother of John, the son of Zebedee; he appears again in Acts 12:20-23, where after failing to give glory to God, he is eaten by worms and dies (a splendid cautionary tale). Herod Agrippa I is succeeded, eventually, by his son, Herod Agrippa II (not much variety in names), who, along with his sisters Drucilla and Berenice, appears later in Acts. Paul attempted to convince Agrippa II of Jesus's lordship (Acts 26) but failed; in 66, the leaders of the First Revolt against Rome succeeded in exiling Agrippa II from Jerusalem. He had no successor.

Although the priests are in charge of the Temple, the passersby reference the Temple in their mocking: "You who would destroy the temple and build it in three days, save yourself, and come down from the cross!" (Mark 15:29-30). Did Jesus speak against the Temple? At the Sanhedrin trial, according to Mark 14:56, people gave "false testimony" or "false witness" against Jesus and that the testimonies did not agree. Among what Mark labels "false witness" is the charge: "We heard him say, 'I will destroy this temple that is made with hands, and in three days I will build another, not made with hands'" (Mark 14:58; see also Matthew 26:61 and Acts 6:14 for variations on this saying).

Friends, we have a problem in sorting out the various testimonies. In John 2:19, following the Fourth Gospel's version of the Temple incident, Jesus states, "Destroy this temple, and in three days I will raise it up." Mark has one version of the saying as false; John has another version of the saying as true. *Oy vey* (a Yiddish interjection; a good expression to know). It seems likely to me that Jesus did say something about the Temple; Jeremiah had done the same centuries before, when the Kingdom of Judah was under threat by the Babylonian Empire. The prophet asked, "Has this house, which is called by my name, become a den of robbers in your sight? You know, I too am watching, says the LORD" (Jeremiah 7:11). The line is worth retweeting.

Josephus, our first-century historian as well as a priest who knew the Temple firsthand, reports that a fellow named "Jesus" [it was not an uncommon name], son of Ananias, predicted the Temple's destruction (*Jewish War* 6.300-309). The local Roman authorities concluded that he was insane; during the First Revolt, he was hit by a catapulted stone and died. The people who wrote several of the Dead Sea Scrolls rejected the Temple because they found its leadership—appointed first by King Herod the Great and then by the Roman governor—illegitimate. Further, the Gospels were all written after the destruction of the Temple, which for them confirmed Jesus's critique. Thus, Mark gives us another example of irony: the Sanhedrin thinks that they are hearing from false witnesses, but this charge is true: Jesus may well have spoken against the Temple.

For the majority of the Jewish population, in Judea and Galilee as well as the Diaspora, the Temple was a place of pilgrimage.

While God was everywhere and so could be worshipped everywhere, the Temple held a special sanctity because it was God's house (see Luke 2:49). It was also a symbol of the nation, so beloved that during the Second Revolt against Rome in 132-135, the Jewish general Bar Kokhba minted coins depicting the Temple.

For many of Jesus's initial followers, all Jews, Temple worship was consistent with Eucharistic celebrations. So too, today, people can attend a church service on Sunday morning and be part of a prayer circle or Bible study on Wednesday evening. Paul participates in Temple worship (see, e.g., Acts 21:23-26); in Romans 9:4, Paul speaks of the perpetual covenantal promises to Israel: "They are Israelites, and to them belong the adoption, the glory, the covenants, the giving of the law, the worship, and the promises." *Worship* here means the Temple service.

For others of Jesus's followers, and many more after 70 when Rome destroyed the Temple, Jesus becomes the new temple. The sacrifices offered by the priests in Jerusalem become first supplemented and then replaced by his final sacrifice in dying on the cross. Already Paul suggests the fluidity of the Temple's identity; he claims that "we [i.e., the members of the assembly in Corinth] are the temple of the living God" (2 Corinthians 6:16). The Epistle to the Hebrews locates Jesus both as ultimate high priest serving at the heavenly altar and as its final sacrifice. Thus, the universalizing church moves away from a national focus, represented by the Temple in Jerusalem, to a spiritual one. As the church becomes increasingly Gentile, the original concerns for the Temple, Jerusalem, and the land of Israel will fade.

Matthew, using Mark as a source, rewrites the verses concerning the Temple: first, Matthew includes the "elders" along with the chief priests and scribes; second, Matthew makes a small but momentous shift in wording. Whereas Mark 15:29-30 has these witnesses say, "You who would destroy the temple and build it in three days, save yourself, and come down from the cross!" Matthew 27:40 rephrases, "You who would destroy the temple and build it in three days, save yourself! If you are the Son of God, come down from the cross." We have heard the challenge, "If you are the Son of God," before. That is how Satan speaks to Jesus. In Matthew 4:3 (also Luke 4:3), the "tempter" says to Jesus, "If you are the Son of God, command these stones to become loaves of bread"; in Matthew 4:6 (also Luke 4:9), he says, "If you are the Son of God, throw yourself down; for it is written, / 'He will command his angels concerning you,' / and 'On their hands they will bear you up, / so that you will not dash your foot against a stone.'"

The bystanders, in Matthew's Gospel, take on the role of Satan. They tempt Jesus to choose to save himself rather than drink the cup prepared for him and die to save others. In the background is the concern for physical pain, be it from fasting or exposure, exhaustion or asphyxiation. People have a choice: we can side with Satan and take the easy road, or we can side with God and know that the road will be difficult. We also need to be careful here, lest we demonize people. Matthew's rephrasing is, on the level of literary artistry, brilliant. In terms of loving both neighbors and enemies, describing people as taking the role of Satan is dangerous.

As for the Temple, Paul presupposes that it will play a role in the working out of the end-times (the technical term for which is *eschatology*). In 2 Thessalonians 2:4, the apostle (or perhaps someone writing in Paul's name, for scholars debate the authenticity of this Epistle) writes of the "man of lawlessness," the "son of perdition," that "He opposes and exalts himself above every so-called god or object of worship, so that he takes his seat in the temple of God, declaring himself to be God."

We need an entire session on the Thessalonian correspondence. For now, we can note that Paul, who wrote before the

Jerusalem Temple was destroyed, thought that the Temple (we cannot be sure he meant the one in Jerusalem, but that seems likely) would be part of the eschatological scenario. (This verse is one of the many reasons why some Christians are convinced that a third temple [the first, built by King Solomon, was destroyed by the Babylonians in 586 BCE; the second, begun following the repatriation of the exiles from Babylon to Judea by Cyrus of Persia in 538, was substantially rebuilt by Herod the Great, with the renovations continuing through the first half of the first century] must be built. There's a major problem with this scenario).

Today, in Jerusalem, a mosque, the Dome of the Rock, stands where the first and second Temples stood. Some people, Jewish and Christian alike, anticipate a third temple. Others shudder at the idea, given the concern Muslims have to protect their own house of worship. Mosques have been built on land where churches once stood, and churches occupy spaces that once were homes to mosques; both churches and mosques stand on the land where at one time synagogues stood. We do well to know the history of the buildings and of the land where we worship. We also do well to consider which biblical predictions we anticipate being fulfilled and which we relegate to the back of the canon or the back of our minds.

The passersby are concerned about the Temple. Mark, likely writing after the destruction of the Temple in 70, sees in Jesus's Temple comments and actions a prediction of its destruction. Jesus may have predicted the Temple's destruction; had he done so, he would have been echoing Jeremiah, who predicted the destruction of the first Temple half a millennium before.

In turn, this echo helps us understand why Jesus may have spoken against the Temple. Jesus did not condemn the Temple because he thought it exploited the poor (the Temple worked on a sliding scale; it was a place where both rich and poor could express fidelity to God). Nor was Jesus concerned about standards of ritual purity. Jesus himself spends time restoring people to states of ritual purity. Nor again was Jesus concerned that the Gentiles were restricted to the outer court since he restricted his own mission to Jews. Rather, Jesus's concern may well have been the same as that voiced by Jeremiah: worshippers who go through the motions but neither repent in their hearts nor act with love of neighbor and love of stranger. Ritual without repentance, financial contribution without fellowship and community, prayer without action, "faith without works" is dead (James 2:26).

## The Cry of Dereliction

Jesus's "cry of dereliction" (another technical term), which Mark gives in Aramaic and then the Greek translation, is the first line of Psalm 22: "My God, my God, why have you forsaken me?" The citation has multiple meanings, from its Aramaic language to its allusion to the rest of Psalm 22, to the role of lament Psalms, to the mistakes of the bystanders who hear Jesus cry.

Mark occasionally depicts Jesus as speaking in Aramaic. For example, to the little girl whom he raises, Jesus says, "Talitha cum," which, Mark tells us, means, "Little girl, get up!" (Mark 5:41). In Mark 7:34, Jesus heals a man who is deaf: "Looking up to heaven, he sighed and said to him, 'Ephphatha,' that is, 'Be opened.'" (When I first typed this line, I wrote "he signed and said...”; thus, I had Jesus fluent in sign language.) In Gethsemane, Jesus prays, "Abba, Father"—the translation is correct; "Abba" means "father," not "daddy"—for you all things are possible; remove this cup from me; yet, not what I want, but what you want" (Mark 14:36). The Aramaic signals at least two things. On the aesthetic level, Aramaic in Greek (or English) texts sounds like we are getting closer to what Jesus actually said, even as it reminds us that we are reading a translation. More, the psalm was originally written not in Aramaic but in Hebrew, so Jesus himself appears engaged in an act of translation.

Second, in Mark's Gospel, Aramaic terms occur, as we've seen, in the contexts of healing. Aramaic words lead a dead child to life and a deaf man to hearing. Perhaps the Aramaic sounded to Greek-attuned ears like a magical incantation. One reputed origin of "hocus pocus" is that it comes from the Latin Mass, when the priest recites, *Hoc est enim corpus meum* ("This is my body"). I've also read that "abracadabra" comes from an Aramaic (!) expression meaning "I create like the word." Consequently, Jesus's Aramaic cry reminds us that when Jesus spoke Aramaic earlier, death and silence are not the end of the story; those who have ears to hear will hear the good news.

The verse Jesus cites is the opening of Psalm 22. Had the witnesses at the cross heard those words correctly, they would have recognized Jesus's ongoing relationship with God. Psalm 22 is conventional; it is one of several "psalms of the lament of an individual"—another is Psalm 69, which also informs the report of the Crucifixion—and it follows a typical pattern: the lamenter expresses the problem ("Why have you forsaken me?"); praises God and reminds God of past actions of salvation ("You are holy"; you saved our ancestors); engages in self-deprecation to gain God's sympathy ("I am a worm"; other people mock me); asks God to help ("save me"; "deliver me"); and offers God an incentive ("I will tell of your name to my brothers and sisters"; "All the ends of the earth shall remember and turn to the LORD"). To pray a "lament" is to be in communication with the divine; faith and hope are not lost. To the contrary, lament psalms reinforce faith, hope, and relationship.

A lament means that even though the divine presence feels absent, we know that God is listening. To lament is a way of arguing with God, of saying, "What is happening is not right; what is happening is a sign not of your justice but of the triumph of sin, or Satan." Abraham argued with God, Moses argued with God, Job argued with God, and numerous psalms have the form of lament. I've had my moments, and you may have too. There is nothing sinful or shameful in speaking out about pain or injustice. There is nothing sinful or shameful in lamenting to God, "I am weary with my crying, / my throat is parched. / My eyes grow dim / with waiting for my God" (Psalm 69:3).

Often, it helps.

Jesus prays, "*My* God, *my* God." The possessive reinforces the relationship rather than questions it. Jesus prays, "My *God*, my *God*," whereas earlier he had addressed God as "Father" (for example, the address to Abba, "Father," in Gethsemane). The terms "Father" and "God" have different connotations. The former seems more imminent, the latter more transcendent. How we address the divine will depend on our needs, and we have multiple addresses to use.

Perhaps this sense of distance, in the shift from "Father" to "God," is one of the reasons why Luke's Gospel omits the cry of dereliction. Instead, in reference to the soldiers if not to all the witnesses at the cross, Jesus prays, "Father, forgive them" (Luke 23:34; the verse is absent from some early manuscripts and it may be a scribal import from Acts 7:60, Stephen's speech). Further, only in Luke does Jesus die with the words "Father, into your hands I commend my spirit" (Luke 23:46). In Luke's version, Jesus dies supported by the loving Father. We can imagine Jesus dying alone, hoping against hope that death is not the end, with a lament psalm on his lips. Or we can imagine him, dying, and knowing that friends are near him, knowing that his messages have not gone unheard or unheeded.

Concerning Mark's narrative: whether Jesus had any hope left depends on how we readers understand his death. Many commentators insist that Jesus felt abandoned. Jesus knew he was going to die. Jesus had pleaded with God, "Remove this cup from me" (Mark 14:36). He has been flagellated, force-marched in a state so weakened he could not carry the crossbeam, stripped naked, nailed to a cross, and exposed to the elements even as everyone around him tormented him. His breathing is increasingly difficult, and each breath causes more pain. He is dying. The words of the psalm, for all their connotations of faith, are real words. He feels deserted. He feels abandoned.

And yet, he did say, more than once, that his death was not the end of his story. In his first Passion prediction, Jesus teaches his disciples "that the Son of Man must undergo great suffering, and be rejected by the elders, the chief priests, and the scribes, and be killed, and after three days rise again" (Mark 8:31). Luke similarly has Jesus describe how "after they have flogged him, they will kill him, and on the third day he will rise again" (Luke 18:33); how "the Son of Man must be handed over to sinners, and be crucified, and on the third day rise again" (Luke 24:7); and how "the Messiah [Greek: *christos*] is to suffer and to rise from the dead on the third day" (Luke 24:46). (By the way, there is no text from the Scriptures of Israel that makes this explicit prediction. Luke gives the impression that Jesus's own statements have scriptural authority.)

We can have numerous assurances of life after death, of resurrection, of peace. When the time comes between life and death, will we believe them, or will we doubt? Is the opening verse of Psalm 22 the end of the story, or the beginning? The Jewish and Christian traditions insist, with assurance and in various ways, that death is not the end of the story.

## The Cup of Sour Wine

After describing how the soldiers brought Jesus to Golgotha, Mark mentions that "they offered him wine mixed with myrrh; but he did not take it" (Mark 15:23). This drink might have been an analgesic for dulling the pain he would endure. Jesus refuses. Perhaps Mark wants us to think of his comment at the Last Supper, "Truly [Greek: *amen*] I tell you, I will never again drink of the fruit of the vine until that day when I drink it new in the kingdom of God" (Mark 14:25). Here again Jesus gives his disciples, and Mark gives readers, the assurance that the cross is not the end of the story.

In Matthew's rewrite, the drink is wine mixed with "gall" or "bile"; Jesus tastes it and then refuses to drink (Matthew 27:34). Matthew may have replaced an act of mercy with an act of malice. To give a dying man something to ease the pain is a kindness; to suggest kindness but then take one more step to increase the pain is appalling.

As the minutes tick on, Mark reports that after Jesus's cry, "someone ran, filled a sponge with sour wine, put it on a stick, and gave it to him to drink, saying, 'Wait, let us see whether Elijah will come to take him down'" (Mark 15:36). This cup of wine, like so much else in this scene, has both historical and theological implications. On the historical register: the wine is a vinegary (hence "sour") mix, here likely the soldiers' drink. The reference to the stick indicates that Jesus is too high up for this unnamed individual (soldier? bystander?) to bring a cup to his lips. He is literally "lifted up."

The wine may also be an allusion to another lament psalm: Psalm 69:21 reads, "They gave me poison for food, / and for my thirst they gave me vinegar to drink." There could even be another nod to Psalm 22:15, "My mouth is dried up like a potsherd, / and my tongue sticks to my jaws." While we can interpret this gesture as one small bit of kindness shown by the people at the cross, given Mark's insistence that everyone mocked Jesus—the soldiers, the bystanders, the chief priests and elders, the other two men being crucified with him—that conclusion is doubtful. Nor does Jesus drink the wine. He gives a loud cry, and then he dies.

Ironically, I have just spent more time describing the agony of the cross than the Gospels do. For the Gospels of Mark and Matthew, the focus is less on the physical pain than it is on the psychological pain caused by taunting, rejection, helplessness, and inevitable death.

For Mark, Jesus dies mocked, deserted, and defeated. Conversely, for John, Jesus is in control, reigning from the cross on which he is lifted up. After insisting on mutual care between his mother and his Beloved Disciple (see chapters 4 and 5), Jesus prepares for his death.

John tells us, "A jar full of sour wine was standing there" (19:29). Yes, this would be something the soldiers might have had, but for John's narrative, the jar of wine appears present as if it were a prop waiting to fulfill prophecy. (Alas, the term for this jar is not the same term as the "water jar" that the Samaritan woman leaves at the well [John 4:28], but I do like the connection.) The notice gives another nod to Psalm 69, cited in relation to the vinegary drink. At times, Gospel writers take a verse out of context; at other times, we do well to look at the full section from which the verse derives. Just as all of Psalm 22 underlies the Crucifixion narrative, so does all of Psalm 69, another psalm of the lament of an individual. This psalm begins, "Save me, O God" (69:1). The psalmist details the enmity of others: "More in number than the hairs of my head / are those who hate me without cause.../ my enemies who accuse me falsely" (69:4). He pleads on behalf of others in a way that Jesus's early followers could see themselves, "Do not let those who hope in you be put to shame because of me" (69:6), and so on. When we review this psalm, we find another familiar verse, as if John were saying, "I told you this psalm was important." Psalm 69:9 reads, "It is zeal for your house that has consumed me": John cited this verse, in chapter 2, in relation to the Temple scene. John 2:17 reads, "His disciples remembered that it was written, 'Zeal for your house will consume me.'"

John continues, "So they put a sponge full of the wine on a branch of hyssop and held it to his mouth" (John 19:29). The reference to a hyssop branch sends us to Exodus 12:22a, the directions on what the Israelite slaves should do with the blood of the lamb they had sacrificed on the eve of their escape from Egypt. Moses instructs, "Take a bunch of hyssop, dip it in the blood that is in the basin, and touch the lintel and the two doorposts with the blood in the basin." In John's Gospel, Jesus is "the Lamb of God who takes away the sin of the world" (John 1:29; cf. 1:36), and he dies, in John's chronology, when the Passover lambs are being sacrificed in the Temple.

Jesus is the Fourth Gospel's new temple. John had already told us this. To the Samaritan woman's question about the proper site of worship, Mount Gerizim in Samaria or Mount Zion in Jerusalem, Jesus responds, "Woman, believe me, the hour is coming when you will worship the Father neither on this mountain nor in Jerusalem." He continues, "But the hour is coming, and is now here, when the true worshipers will worship the Father in spirit and truth, for the Father seeks such as these to worship him" (John 4:21, 23).

At this point, you may well be getting the impression that every word in John sends us to another text, and another nuance, and another theological insight. You would be correct.

John reports, "When Jesus knew that all was now finished, he said (in order to fulfill the Scripture), 'I am thirsty'" (John 19:28). In the Synoptics, while Jesus says nothing about his thirst, the bystanders or soldiers offer him sour wine, which he refuses. Here in John, Jesus says, "I am thirsty," "I thirst." This single word in Greek is his penultimate statement in the Gospel.

"I thirst" first echoes several psalms: "My soul thirsts for God, / for the living God" (Psalm 42:2); "O God, you are my God, I seek you, / my soul thirsts for you" (Psalm 63:1). Along with these theological concerns, there are also anthropological ones, for Jesus, as the divine incarnate, thirsts to be in connection with humanity and to draw humanity to himself. When he says to the Samaritan woman, "Give me a drink" (John 4:7), he is speaking about more than running water; he is wanting to be in communion with her and to give her living water. "I thirst," and Jesus shows a life marked by need. He thirsts, and others need to quench that thirst. He wants others to thirst for him. And, unlike in the Synoptic account, Jesus drinks the wine that is given to him. John 19:30 reports, "When Jesus had received the wine, he said, 'It is finished.'" And then he dies. His last act is receiving the wine that others had given to him.

John's Gospel works to change the way we understand language and so to change the way we understand our lives. "Wind" becomes "Spirit"; "running water" becomes "living water"; light and dark have cosmic implications; any hour can become *the* hour when time and space become renewed. The next time we feel thirsty, will we think of iced tea or living water? When we think of wine (or, for some, grape juice), will we think of a gift given to another who searches for communion with others? John reshapes our language and so reshapes our world.

At the end of John's account, after Jesus takes the drink, he utters his final words: "It is finished." Then "he bowed his head and gave up his spirit" (John 19:30). His spirit? His Spirit? Ancient Greek does not distinguish capital from lowercase letters. The spirit could be the Spirit. The Holy Spirit may have been with Jesus the entire time, another witness at the cross. The Spirit, like the wind, is everywhere, although we do not always notice it. Inhale and exhale, breathe, and feel not just your lungs, your *pneuma* (as in pneumonia or pneumatic), but feel the Spirit, which is what the Greek word *pneuma* means. And we also wait, for in the next chapter of John's Gospel, Jesus will bestow this Spirit on his disciples. But that is another story.

# The King of the Jews

Mark 15:26 mentions that the inscription on the *titulus*, the marker that identified the crime for which the victim suffered, read, "The King of the Jews" (see also Matthew 27:37; Luke 23:38). The titulus indicates that Jesus dies on the charge of sedition, not blasphemy or speaking against the Temple. Thus, his death is a warning to all passersby—local or from the Diaspora: this is what Rome does to any who challenge, or are perceived to be challenging, the empire.

Only in John's Gospel does the titulus become a controversial matter. According to John's elaboration, the title is not simply "King of the Jews" but "Jesus of Nazareth [or, Nazorean], the King of the Jews" (19:19). John adds Jesus's name and hometown. Let there be no mistake: for Pilate, the title is meant to humiliate both Jesus and his fellow Jews. For Pilate, Rome, not popular support, appoints kings. But for John's readers, Jesus of Nazareth, and Jesus of Nazareth only, is the king of the Jews. The title is correct, although Pilate and his soldiers do not know this. Artistic depictions with the letters I.N.R.I. on the titulus follow John's Gospel. The letters derive from the Latin (Jerome's Vulgate) translation: *Iesus Nazarenus Rex Iudaeorum*.

John records, "Many of the Jews read this inscription, because the place where Jesus was crucified was near the city; and it was written in Hebrew, in Latin, and in Greek" (John 19:20). With this line, John adds to the list of passersby. The verse gives me pause. The historian in me wonders how many people could read. While the level of literacy among the Jewish population may have been higher than the empire-wide average, it was still not high. We only have good rates of literacy with the rise of public schools.

The politically aware part of me thinks of how in many locations signs appear in more than one language (with English usually included). In other places, people have attempted to restrict the public use of foreign languages with the cry, "If they want to live here, let them learn..." Pontius Pilate thus becomes a representative of multiculturalism and international welcome. Who knew? I once proposed to use this verse regarding multiple translations in support of teaching foreign language in the public school system; my friends suggested that the support would be limited since Pilate is not a great role model.

Other questions surface in reading the Fourth Gospel's account. We read about "many Jews." How many Jews saw this sign and lamented that Rome was again executing one of their own people? Did they stop, or did they continue doing whatever they had planned? Do we read a sign—a billboard, or a sign in a person's hands—and drive on? Do we hear of another death and then go on with our day? Or does one person's death change everything? When do we notice?

The "chief priests of the Jews" knew about the sign, and they attempted to change the wording. They tell Pilate, "Do not write, 'The King of the Jews,' but, 'This man said, I am King of the Jews.'" Pilate denies the request with a terse, "What I have written I have written" (John 19:21-22). The move to change the sign is not a practical one: "many Jews" had already seen it. I am reminded of politicians, athletes, and movie stars who attempt to walk back what they have said or posted. There are enough tapes or screenshots to show their hypocrisy. The chief priests are showing their desperation.

It would not be the first time. When Pilate had asked the chief priests at Jesus's trial, "Shall I crucify your king?" they respond, "We have no king but the emperor [Greek: *Caesar*]" (John 19:15). With the titulus, Pilate mocks the chief priests. But that earlier scene opens another question: Who is the ultimate, rightful king? The answer "Caesar"—or any political authority—is never the right answer.

Ironically (so much in John's narrative is ironic), Jesus *never claimed* to be "King of the Jews." To the contrary, after Jesus had fed the five thousand (the one miracle story in all four canonical Gospels), in John's account, "When Jesus realized that they were about to come and take him by force to make him king, he withdrew again to the mountain by himself" (John 6:15). He could have taken the throne of this world had he wanted it; he did not. His enthronement, his being "lifted up," for John, is his Crucifixion.

To the contrary again, when Pilate asked him about being "King of the Jews" (John 18:33), Jesus responded, "My kingdom is not from this world…my kingdom is not from here" (John 18:36). The statement raises questions about Constantine gaining an empire under the sign of the cross, and of nation-states with crosses on their flags. To what extent should church and state be mutually implicated? If Jesus is not a king in an earthly political sense, why do some of his followers want their political systems to be "Christian" ones? Are disciples to be "in the world but not of it," or are followers to "love the world" as God so did and do their best to create a heaven on earth?

## Chief Priests, Scribes, and Elders

Mark's account emphasizes Jesus's utter humiliation and abandonment: passersby, chief priests and scribes, and the two men crucified with him all question, in distinct ways, his messianic status. For the chief priests and scribes, the taunting concerns Jesus's messianic status and the role of belief. After describing the taunts by others, Mark 15:31-32 reports, "In the same way the chief priests, along with the scribes, were also mocking him among themselves and saying, 'He saved others; he cannot save himself. Let the Messiah [Greek: *christos*], the King of Israel, come down from the cross now, so that we may see and believe.'"

With these lines, Mark brings the hostility Jesus faced from the scribes and chief priests full circle. As early as 2:6-7, Mark records that after Jesus told the paralyzed man, "Son, your sins are forgiven," "Some of the scribes were sitting there, questioning in their hearts, 'Why does this fellow speak in this way? It is blasphemy! Who can forgive sins but God alone?'" This same concern for blasphemy reappears at the Sanhedrin trial, where Jesus acknowledges that he is the "Messiah [Greek: *christos*], the Son of the Blessed One" and the chief priests accuse him of blasphemy (see Mark 14:61-64). The charges, throughout, are false, but a false charge can nevertheless help us to think about actual concerns.

The first false charge is that Jesus forgives the paralyzed man's sins. Technically, he does not. Rather, using what grammarians call the "divine passive," he states that the sins were forgiven. Had he done the forgiving himself, he would have said, "I forgive you."

Second, to call oneself a child of God is not blasphemous. Luke's genealogy describes Adam as a "son of God" (Luke 3:38), and so, by extension, every one of us can claim the designation. We are all children of God. The high priest's charge of blasphemy is just as false as the other charges brought against Jesus.

The concern for blasphemy, although a false charge in the Gospel, raises several contemporary concerns. In some countries, today, blasphemy is a capital crime, and in many others (you can look these up; you may be surprised) blasphemy is a punishable offense. The first question: Can we recognize blasphemy when we hear it? For example, to talk about the "angry, wrathful, tribal God of the Old Testament" versus the "merciful, loving, universal God of the New Testament" is blasphemy: that was the view of the second-century heretic Marcion. Yet this image is still common in many a church today. Is using the expression "Jesus Christ" to express exasperation blasphemous? What about "godd---" (or, the southern spoonerism variant, "dadgum," which I heard for the first time when I moved to North Carolina to do graduate work at Duke)? Some of us still get concerned with profanity: is blasphemy on the same register as those words that you all know, but that I prefer not to type?

Next, should there be laws against blasphemy? Should there be sanctions against people who use an image of Jesus in an obscene way as some cartoonists have done with images of the prophet Muhammad?

The chief priests and scribes, who accused Jesus of blasphemy, now taunt Jesus in a way that shows the limitations of translation. They acknowledge, "He saved others." With this statement, they confirm their awareness of Jesus's miracles. This point is clear in the Greek text, but most English translations mask it. When Jairus begs Jesus to heal his daughter, he says, "Come and lay your hands on her, so that she may *be saved* and live" (Mark 5:23), emphasis added, emphasis added; most English translations offer "so that she may be made well." Similarly, the woman suffering from hemorrhages thinks, "If I but touch his clothes, I will *be saved*" (Mark 5:28); again, English versions offer "be made well." When Jesus heals this woman, he tells her, "Daughter, your faith has saved you (English: "made you well"); go in peace, and be healed of your disease" (Mark 5:34).

The taunts of the chief priests and elders help us to see the varied meanings of the term *saved*. We may think of salvation as something that happens after we die or following the final judgment. For Jesus and his early followers, that's one possible meaning. In Israel's Scriptures, being "saved" usually means not an end-of-life or end-of-time situation; it means being rescued from whatever ills beset us today: slavery in Egypt, exile in Babylon, famine or plague, threats of war, death from disease. The act of saving can be the entry of the divine into history, but it can also be a human act: of healing, of protection, of economic support, of peacemaking. Saving is something that is not restricted to the divine; saving is something we can do.

Saving is something also that we can feel: recovery from an illness, safety after an accident. I have heard students say more than once, "That extra study session saved me from failing," or, for me, less celebratory, "She was going to ask me to translate this sentence, but I was saved by the bell."

The chief priests and scribes say, "He cannot save himself.... come down from the cross now, so that we may see and believe." They are thinking of salvation in terms of rescue from death. They have missed the fact that in the Gospels, salvation is not simply a rescue from present danger; it is also the state of a right relationship between humanity and divinity. The first time the Greek word meaning "saved" appears in the New Testament is Matthew 1:21, the angel's message to Joseph concerning Mary's pregnancy: "She will bear a son, and you are to name him Jesus, for he will save his people from their sins." The name *Jesus* derives from a Hebrew root that means "salvation." To sin is to create alienation, whether between people (you sin against me; I sin against you) or between humanity and divinity (we sin against God).

Jewish teaching recognizes that people will sin; the Torah provides several mechanisms for restoring relationship: atonement by individuals and by the community, restitution, sacrifice, and so on. Jesus, for his followers, not only prompts people to atone—hence his meals with tax collectors and sinners; he's not at the table just for gourmet dining—but also offers his life as a mechanism for that atonement. Matthew and Mark state that he dies as "a ransom for many" (Matthew 20:28 // Mark 10:45).

To restrict the idea of salvation to a personal postmortem status means to ignore the role of salvation in relation to slavery, sickness, exile, or despair; such restriction of meaning is to fail to acknowledge human need for help and human gratitude when it comes. Salvation cannot just be eschatological. But to ignore the need humanity has for reconciliation is to ignore the importance of community and, in the Christian tradition, of the cross. Indeed, the chief priests and scribes, in their taunting, preclude both community and reconciliation. Mark (15:31) tells us that they "were also mocking him among themselves"—among themselves. They do not talk to Jesus, and they do not talk to the passersby. They have isolated themselves from community rather than promoted reconciliation.

Jesus states, "For those who want to save their life will lose it, and those who lose their life for my sake, and for the sake of the gospel, will save it" (Mark 8:35). When the chief priests and scribes say, "Let the Messiah [Greek: *christos*], the King of Israel, come down from the cross now, so that we may see and believe" (Mark 15:32), they are misreading Jesus's message. To "see and believe" requires seeing the death of Jesus and believing that this death is not the end of the story. Jesus must lose his life to gain it, for himself and, according to the Gospels, for everyone else.

Finally, when the chief priests and scribes taunt Jesus to come down so that they may see and believe, they get Mark's Christology—the understanding of who the Christ is and what he does—backward. In Mark's Gospel, belief is not based on seeing a miracle. To the contrary, Mark states flatly that in Nazareth, Jesus's hometown, Jesus "could do no deed of power there, except that he laid his hands on a few sick people and cured them" (Mark 6:5). The point is understated since I'd take healing the sick to be a fine deed of power. For Mark, belief comes before the miracle, not after. More, belief for Mark is to be based not in the witnessing of mighty works but in the witnessing of the Crucifixion. Mark's Christology is not about miracles; it is about suffering and dying as a ransom. To go to church for the show, for the deeds of power, is to miss Mark's point.

The chief priests and scribes, who have clearly missed the point (missed the Mark?), ironically fulfill one more prophetic statement. They tell Jesus to escape the nails fixing him to the cross so that they will see and believe. The comment echoes Jesus's statement about why he teaches in parables, "in order that they may indeed look, but not perceive" (Mark 4:12), a citation from Isaiah 6:9-10. The parable, the mystery of the life and death of Jesus, is opaque to them.

## And Now?

The chief priests, elders, scribes, and leaders are absent from John's Gospel. Only in the Gospels of Mark and Matthew does Jesus cry the first line of Psalm 22, and only in these two Gospels do the people at the cross think he is calling Elijah. In Matthew and Mark, the bystanders taunt Jesus; in Luke some are his supporters; in John, they are absent. Our major concern is not to question the historicity of the events (although I admit that the historian in me does have questions). The major concern is sorting what the Evangelists prompt us to notice, urge us to question, and suggest that we learn. Elijah has already come, twice: first in the figure of John the Baptist and second at the Transfiguration. Would we recognize him if we saw him? What tells us that the messianic age is beginning?

## Chapter Two

# THE OTHER VICTIMS

For more than twenty years, I have been teaching Vanderbilt Divinity School courses at Riverbend Maximum Security Institute (RMSI; we call it "Riverbend"). My divinity students and I drive to the prison, pass the various security checkpoints, and then hold class together with twelve to fifteen insider students. More often than not, the insiders ask the hard questions that the free-world folks from Vanderbilt, many planning on entering Christian ministry, need to consider: sentencing and parole, repentance and forgiveness, trust and protection. The insider students ask: "What were the stories of the two men who died with Jesus—what did they do? What were the circumstances that condemned them to death?" The insider students wonder: "Who cared for their bodies? Where were their friends? What were their names?" And they ask these ministers-to-be, "Do you remind your congregations that Jesus told the sheep at the final judgment, 'I was in prison and you visited me' (Matthew 25:36b)?"

I have also held classes, not sponsored by Vanderbilt, with men on death row. Sometimes, in one-on-one conversations, I would talk about a biblical text with men who spend twenty-three of twenty-four hours in a small cell; sometimes we could meet in a group around a table, with the guards not far away. They, too, had questions, even more pressing ones, about life and death, and the afterlife, about hope and despair. We once did a Passover seder on death row: there was no matzah and no wine, no bitter herbs and no hard-boiled egg. But we did have *haggadahs*, the text that recounts the story of the Exodus. We read the story, prayed the prayers, and sang the songs. But only I and my good friend Rev. David Phillipy (who has since died, may his memory be for a blessing) left the building. I cried on the way home, for I sensed a freedom, a palpable sense of freedom, that the other men at that seder table, would never have.

I cannot read the Gospel accounts of the two men crucified with Jesus and not think about my friends at Riverbend. My concern here is not to sentimentalize my insider students. Nor am I speaking about forgiving them for the crimes they have committed, since that is not my call. Only the victims and their loved ones impacted by the crimes have this right. Rather, my insider students have taught me, repeatedly, that they are individuals with families and friends, with stories of how they came to be sentenced to prison, with guilt and remorse. As one remarked, and here I am paraphrasing, "We are individuals, not just 'the rapist' or 'the murderer.' God-forbid that you would be known by the worst thing you ever did. We are human beings, just like you, in the image and likeness of God." My insider students are my friends; the witnesses at the cross force us all to notice them, and to remember them.

Mark 15:22 (see also Matthew 27:33) describes the initial events at Jesus's crucifixion: "They [the soldiers] brought Jesus to the place called Golgotha..." Five verses later, Mark announces, "And with [Jesus] they crucified two *bandits*, one on his right and one on his left" (Mark 15:27, emphasis added; see also Matthew 27:38). John records the same information in different words: "And carrying the cross by himself, he went out to what is called The Place of the Skull, which in Hebrew is called Golgotha. There they crucified him, and with him two *others*, one on either side, with Jesus between them" (John 19:17-18, emphasis added).

Luke, who was likely following Mark and possibly Matthew, makes two major editorial changes regarding the men crucified with Jesus. First, Luke 23:33, like John, connects the name of the location to the description of the three condemned to death: "When they came to the place that is called The Skull, they crucified Jesus there with the criminals, one on his right and one on his left." Second, only Luke presents a short interchange among the three victims. Luke reports,

> *One of the criminals who were hanged there kept deriding (NRSV: the Greek is literally "blaspheming"] him and saying, "Are you not the Messiah [Greek: christos]? Save yourself and us!" But the other rebuked him, saying, "Do you not fear God, since you are under the same sentence of condemnation? And we indeed have been condemned justly, for we are getting what we deserve for our deeds, but this man has done nothing wrong." Then he said, "Jesus, remember me when you come into your kingdom." He replied, "Truly I tell you, today you will be with me in Paradise."*
>
> *Luke 23:39-43*

With these scenes, the Gospel writers challenge us to address several topics that many of us, myself included, would rather not engage, including the anonymity of so many imprisoned and executed people: the names we forget and the names we never know; the ongoing practices of torture and capital punishment; the horrible things that we say when we are desperate and in pain; and the fear that some of us have of dying, especially if we have not rectified and cannot rectify harm we have done to others. Anyone who says biblical studies is easy, or that all we need is love, is living in a fantasy world. The Bible forces us to ask the hard questions, and it will not let us avert our eyes from sin and guilt. When we pick up the Bible's challenge, we come closer to the group Jesus described when he said, "Blessed are those who hunger and thirst for righteousness, for they will be filled" (Matthew 5:6).

We start with the explicit note in Mark and Matthew of the two men, "one on his right and one on his left," which may be an allusion to Isaiah 53:12b-c, one of the "servant songs," in which God's suffering servant is described in the following terms:

> *"He poured out himself to death,*
> *and was numbered with the transgressors;*
> *yet he bore the sin of many,*
> *and made intercession for the transgressors."*

The Gospel notice could also be an allusion to Psalm 22:16, "A company of evildoers encircle me." On the other hand, Matthew and Mark may well be describing what actually happened.

We then hear from Gestas and Dismas—the names given to these men by tradition and not by the Gospels—directly. Their comments raise for us the pressing question of the crimes for which they are guilty: Are they bandits or thieves, or are they freedom fighters, or are they terrorists? Finally we focus on Luke 23:39-43 and the multiple issues raised by the conversation the three dying men have, a conversation that includes: the "blasphemy" of the first speaker, the connection of his comment to Satan's temptation of Jesus, the importance of the second man's "word of rebuke" in relation to the commandment to "love your neighbor as yourself," the exhortation to "fear God" in light of a concern for the final judgment, the acknowledgment of guilt but also the accepting of punishment (you can bet I'll take issue with his claim that "we are getting what we deserve for our deeds"), and the proclamation of Jesus's righteousness. We'll understand what this penitent, dying man reveals about the *kingdom* Jesus has been proclaiming. And we'll develop the implications of Jesus's promise, "Truly I tell you, today you will be with me in Paradise."

### *"One on his right and one on his left" (Mark 15:27; see also Matthew 27:38; Luke 23:33; John 19:18).*

Jesus dies between two men. This would not have been unusual. Capital punishment in the Roman Empire was often carried out on the bodies of many. Josephus, the first-century Jewish historian, recounts numerous reports of crucifixions: by the Hasmonean king Alexander Jannaeus, who crucified eight hundred Pharisees (*Jewish Antiquities* 13.380), by the Roman general Varus, who crucified two thousand "rebels" who sought to overthrow Roman rule at the death of King Herod the Great in 4 BCE (*Jewish Antiquities* 17.295), and many others. Josephus himself testifies to having seen many people crucified (*The Life* 420) during the first revolt against Rome in 66-70 CE.

There may have been others executed with Jesus that spring day at the time of Passover, but the Gospels point to two men. The references immediately open to multiple interpretations. Here are three.

First, readers of Mark's Gospel will have heard the reference to Jesus's right and left hands earlier. In Mark 10:35, immediately after Jesus tells his disciples, *again*, that he will be mocked, spat upon, flogged, and killed, and then be raised, the sons of Zebedee, James and John, say to Jesus, "Teacher, we want you to do for us whatever we ask of you." What a question! They avoid the references to the Passion, jump right to the Resurrection, and ask for a blank check drawn on the miracle account. Jesus (I sense with some degree of exasperation) asks, "What is it you want me to do for you?" At this point, the disciples should have asked for "world peace" (if you've seen the movie *Miss Congeniality* with Sandra Bullock, you will know the importance of this concern), or perhaps a cure for Alzheimer's, given the concern for memory that surfaces in the story of Jesus's execution and, for me personally, given that this horrible disease is slowly taking away parts of my wonderful mother-in-law's sense of place and sense of self. There are numerous things we might ask for, if given such a blank check.

The two disciples, still not at their best, ask, "Grant us to sit, one at your right hand and one at your left, in your glory" (Mark 10:37). Apparently, Jesus's numerous messages about servant leadership, the first being last, the importance of humility, and so on did not take root. Jesus responds that "to sit at my right hand or at my left is not mine to grant, but it is for those for whom it has been prepared" (Mark 10:40). This is a remarkably calm response; my own comments would likely have been more pointed.

The Gospel then tells us who will be on Jesus's left and right: two other men, dying on two other crosses.

According to Matthew 20:21, it is the boys' *mother* who says to Jesus, "Declare that these two sons of mine will sit, one at your right hand and one at your left, in your kingdom." She is the original helicopter parent.

As Jesus denied the sons' request in Mark's version of this incident, so he denies the mother's request in Matthew's. He does not respond to the mother directly; instead (here following Mark), he turns to her sons to say to them, "You [plural] do not know what you are asking. Are you [plural] able to drink the cup that I am about to drink?" (Matthew 20:22). Compared to Mark's portrait of the disciples (they are not the brightest students in the seminar), Matthew gives the men an upgrade. Now it is not the boys but their mother who appears interested in career advancement.

I love Matthew's retelling. Jesus doesn't ask the woman who she is; I think he knows, because she's been part of the group since the beginning. Perhaps he appreciates that she is kneeling, since she doesn't strike me as a particularly humble person (I'm projecting). Kneeling is a good way both of getting someone's attention and holding one's own ground in the process. Perhaps Jesus also appreciates her style, for Mrs. Zebedee doesn't immediately say what she wants. She asks for a favor.

If we had the chance to ask Jesus a favor, for what would we ask? World peace? Cure for cancer or heart disease? A balanced budget? Racial reconciliation? Mrs. Zebedee goes the more personal route. She is asking not only on behalf of her sons, but on her own behalf as well: "Those are *my boys* up there in the places of honor," she wants to say. The good news is that Mrs. Zebedee is among the few who has an inkling of who Jesus is. The bad news is that she understands his regal role but not his suffering one. The good news is that she recognizes he has a kingdom. The bad news is that she thinks the kingdom is marked by advancement rather than by service.

Were I in the position to advocate for my children, asking for them to have seats of honor would not be high on my wish list. There are better requests we can make for our children: Please Lord, keep them safe; please, protect them from evil; please, guide their steps in the paths of righteousness. Mrs. Zebedee asks the wrong question. The cup that Jesus will drink is the cup of martyrdom. Her son James will be among the first martyrs; the Book of Acts recounts that Herod Agrippa I had him killed him with a sword (Acts 12:2).

John, the other son, is the purported author of the Fourth Gospel; his charge in that Gospel is to take care of the mother of Jesus, which raises the question: Who will care for Mrs. Zebedee? If the Beloved Disciple in the Fourth Gospel is John the son of Zebedee, will he care for the mother of Jesus and his own mother? Will these two women, both of whom lost their sons to state power, find strength in each other's presence?

I understand that mothers can be pushy; sometimes it is better not to push. This is one where the second option is preferable. Mrs. Zebedee (we do not have a name for her) I think got the point (I do like her), as we shall see when we meet her together with the other women at the cross in chapter 5.

Second, Matthew's readers will see another reference to Jesus's right and left hands. In the famous Parable of the Sheep and the Goats, the king "will put the sheep at his right hand and the goats at the left" (Matthew 25:33). Knowing this reference, we may think of the two who die with Jesus as epitomizing the goats (the one who neglected the suffering of Jesus himself) and the sheep (and one who attended to it). One dying man "blasphemes" Jesus; the other defends him.

On the other hand (as it were), if we see the "wicked thief" as a goat and so ignore his own pain, have we joined the goat line ourselves? This posing of difficult questions is what parables are supposed to do (and that is another book).

Third, some manuscripts of Mark make explicit that the execution scene fulfills prophecy. In many New Testament translations, Mark 15:29 follows immediately upon Mark 15:27, as if a verse disappeared. (Check your Bibles; see if you have Mark 15:28.) The rationale for this disappearance is that the editors of many translations concluded that verse 28 was added by scribes to an earlier text. The verse, Mark 15:28, reads, "And the scripture was fulfilled that says, 'And he was counted among the lawless.'" The scripture reference is to Isaiah 53:12, one of the so-called "servant songs" of Isaiah. Isaiah's long verse, which for Jesus's early followers necessarily pointed to him, includes the line, "[He] was numbered with the transgressors; / yet he bore the sin of many, / and made intercession for the transgressors." Luke 22:37 cites this verse but in a different context. Jesus tells his disciples that if they do not have swords, they must purchase them. Why? "For I tell you, this scripture must be fulfilled in me, 'And he was counted among the lawless'; and indeed what is written about me is being fulfilled." This point helps us remember that we are reading translations of translations of copies of copies—we have no original text of any Gospel. It also reminds us that to bear arms can number us "among the lawless." But, resolving the question of Jesus and the Second Amendment to the US Constitution is above my pay grade.

The stories of the two men who die with Jesus provoke questions of honor and service, salvation and damnation, original stories and scribal modifications. And they do so much more. There were likely three, or even more, people who died that morning outside Jerusalem. The stories told of them, and the stories that will continue to be told about them, are not only stories about Jesus, but they are also stories with which we should wrestle, stories of crime and punishment, of anguish and hope, of blasphemy and salvation.

## Thieves, Bandits, Criminals, Evildoers, Terrorists, or Freedom Fighters?

While the NRSV of Luke 23:32-33 calls the two men executed with Jesus "criminals," the Greek term literally means "evildoers." Matthew 27:38 and Mark 15:27 describe them with a Greek term meaning "bandits" or "robbers," the same expression used in the Parable of the Man Waylaid by Robbers (I'm not a fan of the title "Good Samaritan," since it is premised on the idea that most Samaritans are not good) in Luke 10:30 to describe the people who "stripped [the traveler], beat him, and went away, leaving him half dead." The term also appears in Jesus's accusation, "My house shall be called a house of prayer, / but you are making it a den of *robbers*" (Matthew 21:13, emphasis added; cf. Mark 11:17; Luke 19:46), his query to the party that arrested him in Gethsemane, "Have you come out with swords and clubs to arrest me as though I were a *bandit*?" (Matthew 26: 55, emphasis added; cf. Mark 14:48; Luke 22:52), and the "thief and the *bandit*" who steal sheep in John's "Good Shepherd" discourse (John 10:1, 8, emphasis added).). Paul uses the term to describe the dangers he faced, "danger from *bandits*... danger at sea, danger from false brothers" (2 Corinthians 11:26 , emphasis added). The word means "robber" or "bandit."

Nevertheless, some biblical commentators want to see these two men not as robbers in the sense of someone committing a crime, but as freedom fighters or revolutionaries. The reason for this view is, in part, the remaining use of the term in the New Testament. According to John 18:40, Barabbas, the prisoner set free, "was a *bandit*" (emphasis added). Matthew 27:16 calls him a "notorious prisoner." However, Mark 15:7 (cf. Luke 23:19) states that "Barabbas was in prison with the rebels who had committed murder during the insurrection." Reading the term *bandit* as connected to political insurrection gets us not criminals but political revolutionaries. Barabbas becomes Che Guevara.

At this point, my historical antennae go on alert. The Roman Empire was brutal and venal, but on the whole it wasn't stupid. There is no notice outside of the Gospels of governors in Judea freeing someone at the behest of the population; if there were such a thing, it would have been stupid (the technical term) on Pilate's part to offer the crowd an insurrectionist. It seems to me more likely that the story of Barabbas, whose Aramaic name means "son of the father" (the term *abba*, which Jesus uses in Gethsemane, we've already noted) is meant as an allegory. One innocent "Son of the Father" dies in the place of the guilty "son of the father." The historicity of Barabbas is questionable; the theological meaning is profound.

Another reason some scholars promote this connotation of rebel is that they want to make Jesus into a "Zealot," a political revolutionary. He was not. He was an artisan from a small town in the Galilee, who was expecting the inbreaking of divine justice, not the outbreaking of a political revolt.

We do not know what crimes the other two men committed. Yet the question of translation and so connotation prompts difficult questions. Both Tony Soprano and Jean Valjean took what did not belong to them; do we judge them by the same criteria? One man stole in order to make money for himself; the other stole in order to survive. One person's freedom fighter is someone else's terrorist. How do we determine the correct label? Finally, what circumstances might drive a person to become a *bandit*, and what circumstances might have prevented a person from committing a crime?

To steal for one's own personal finances—not to help another, not to reclaim what is rightfully ours—is to sin. When a tax collector overcharges for personal gain, that is stealing. "Do not steal" is one of the Ten Commandments (Exodus 20:15; Leviticus 19:11, 13; Deuteronomy 5:19). John the Baptizer therefore instructs tax collectors not to collect more than the amount of taxes due; he tells soldiers not to extort by threats or false charges (Luke 3:12-14). In other words, the Baptizer tells people not to steal. That's a step in the right direction: name the bad action. Jesus dines with sinners and tax collectors, people who violate the social good by stealing, and encourages them to repent. That's the next step in the right direction: if people who violate social welfare do not come to you, go to them in love, break bread with them, and not simply tell them but show them how to repent and to get back onto the correct path.

### One of the criminals who were hanged there kept deriding him (Luke 23:39a).

The NRSV states that one of these men "derided" Jesus, but the Greek says, "blasphemed." It is the same term, in Greek, that describes the men who were holding Jesus at the home of the high priest, the men who "began to mock him and beat him; they also blindfolded him and kept asking him, 'Prophesy! Who is it that struck you?' They kept heaping many other *insults* on him" (Luke 22:63-65, emphasis added). That last line, in the Greek, reads, "and many other blasphemies they were continuing to speak against him." "Insults" doesn't come close to the level of verbal abuse.

Luke strategically uses this verb only one other place, and here the NRSV gives the literal translation. In Luke 12:10, Jesus states, "Everyone who speaks a word against the Son of Man will be forgiven; but whoever blasphemes against the Holy Spirit will not be forgiven."

We can make several observations about the implications of this word used by the dying man in the context of Luke's Gospel. Here are four.

First, Jesus's preferred self-designation is not "Son of God" (the term that the centurion in Mark and Matthew will use to describe him) but "Son of Man." In making the comment about the Son of Man and the Spirit, Jesus thus makes a distinction between himself and the Spirit. I can understand the distinction. Jesus is now dying the torturous death of a criminal; he is not rescuing himself from death and he is not rescuing the men who will die with him. Thus, doubting Jesus, under the circumstances, would not necessarily be a sign of bad faith. His disciples have heard him promise his resurrection, and even they, who witnessed his miracles, do not believe him. But even if they doubt Jesus's own role, they are not to doubt the Spirit as the manifestation of the divine. They are not to doubt God's ultimate power and God's ultimate justice.

Second, although the Gospels do not present the details, Jesus is being tortured to death. That victims of crucifixion can even find the breath to speak is already remarkable. Gestas, the blaspheming victim, knows of Jesus's reputation. He speaks from his pain and his disappointment. He is completely honest about how he feels, and Luke gives us this glimpse into his despair. Luke also invites readers to speculate: Might we be this honest in our doubts? Can we speak now, or do we express doubt only at the last minute? Can we sympathize, empathize with this victim?

Third, about the soldiers, just following orders, Jesus prays, "Father, forgive them; for they do not know what they are doing" (Luke 23:34). Does this prayer extend to this blaspheming man? Did he know what he was doing when he committed his crimes? Is he the same man now as he was when he committed them (a question to which I continually return in working with my insider students at Riverbend)? Did Jesus pray for him as well?

Finally, in discussing this passage about blasphemy against the Spirit, one of my insider students explained, "Blasphemy against the Holy Spirit is believing that God could not love someone like me." The explanation is worth consideration.

## "Are you not the Messiah? Save yourself and us!" (Luke 23:39b).

According to Mark 15:--32, not only do the chief priests and scribes mock Jesus, so too "Those who were crucified with him also taunted him" (see also Matthew 27:44). Luke extends the scene by putting the taunting on the lips of the man crucified next to Jesus. In stating, "Are you not the Messiah?" he is saying, "Clearly you are not the Messiah. If you were, none of us would be here. If you were, you would *save yourself and us.*" The man is not asking a real question; he is tormenting, blaspheming, Jesus with his comment.

The phrasing of his question resembles the devil's questions to Jesus during the wilderness trial. In the third temptation, according to Luke's order, the devil "took [Jesus] to Jerusalem, and placed him on the pinnacle of the temple." Then, at this precarious place, he tempts, "If you are the Son of God, throw yourself down from here, for it is written, / 'He will command his angels concerning you, / to protect you,' / and / 'On their hands they will bear you up, / so that you will not dash your foot against a stone'" (Luke 4:9-11). The citations are to Psalm 91:11-12. Ironically, in ancient

Jewish literature, including the Jerusalem Talmud (y. Shabbat 8b), the psalm is known as a "song against demons"; citing the psalm, the devil is in effect banishing himself. He was defeated before he started. To the devil Jesus responds, "It is said, 'Do not put the Lord your God to the test'" (Luke 4:12, citing Deuteronomy 6:16). Jesus refuses to act on his own behalf. At the same time, the Gospel is winking at later readers, for those readers know that "Lord your God" refers, for the followers of Jesus, not just to "God the Father" but to Jesus himself.

At the cross, we have a repeat of the temptation: a "doer of evil" says, "If you are the Messiah, prove it by rescuing yourself and me as well." Jesus again refuses to succumb to temptation. Again, Jesus shows what it means to be "led into temptation" and also how to resist it.

Jesus describes his mission as one of saving "the lost" (Luke 19:10). Such saving may require that the lost recognize their condition. The "lost" in the Gospel are the sinners and the tax collectors, the people who put their own welfare ahead of others and who, in what was generally a zero-sum economy, took more so that others had less. By dining with "sinners and tax collectors," the ancient versions of insider traders, human traffickers, drug dealers, and the A-list people who feast while others starve, he called them to repentance, to rejoining the community, to responsibility. Did this fellow even realize that he was lost? Perhaps, after the other dying man speaks to him, he might. The story of this first "evildoer" may not be over. We can choose how to tell his story.

Finally, a note on characterization. When I was an undergraduate at Smith College, one of my English professors commented on the importance of first and last impressions. We were to attend to the first thing a character says, and the last. While sermons on the seven last words of Jesus are common, I've never heard a sermon on this criminal's last words, these words of derision, and this demand for salvation. Yet they still ring in my ears. "Save yourself and us" is a rephrasing of the plea, "Hosanna," which comes from the Hebrew for "save now" or "save, I pray." Since *save* means rescue, how do we save men like this blaspheming thief?

**But the other rebuked him, saying, "Do you not fear God, since you are under the same sentence of condemnation?" (Luke 23:40).**

While the victim known traditionally as Gestas taunts, the victim known as Dismas treats Jesus not only with respect, but with full messianic knowledge of Jesus as King of the Jews and Savior. His words of rebuke to the other dying man and his words of support for and supplication to Jesus perfectly fit into Luke's narrative. In his first comment, Dismas asserts Jesus's innocence, a point Luke—especially compared to Mark and Matthew—emphasizes. The scene thus plays upon the convention that it takes one to know one. The two thieves know they are guilty of the charges against them, and they know Jesus is not.

Luke, and only Luke, stresses Jesus's righteousness and so innocence. Only in Luke does Jesus meet Herod Antipas, and Herod did not condemn him (Luke 23:15 [two times]); three times Pilate finds no guilt in him despite pressure from the high priest (Luke 23:4, 14, 22). Now even a criminal, an "evildoer," finds Jesus innocent. More, he comes to Jesus's defense by insisting: "This man has done nothing wrong" (Luke 23:41); the Greek is *atopos*, which means that Jesus did nothing "out of place" or "improper".

Ironically, and sadly, a stranger defends Jesus when his own disciples do not. Help and support can come from the most unexpected places. Earlier in Luke's Gospel, Jesus told a story about a Samaritan, from a group known for attacking Jewish pilgrims going from Galilee to Judea to worship in the Jerusalem Temple, who stops to help an injured man who is half-dead (or for fans of

*The Princess Bride*, "mostly dead"). Now, an evildoer rebukes his fellow criminal and comes to Jesus's defense while Jesus himself can be seen as "half-dead." The Samaritan, unexpectedly, shows compassion when the priest and Levite in the parable do not; the doer of evil does good when the disciples in the story of Jesus are nowhere to be found. Perhaps the priest and Levite were afraid of bandits on the road; perhaps the disciples were afraid of being rounded up with Jesus. Are the excuses valid?

Luke tells us that the second victim "rebuked" the one who had blasphemed (23:40). In Jewish tradition, "rebuke" or "reprove" or even "convict" is what we are required to do when we see our neighbor doing something wrong. Otherwise, we would be, in modern terms, "aiding and abetting" evildoing. Leviticus 19:18, the famous verse that reads, "You shall not take vengeance or bear a grudge against any of your people, but you shall love your neighbor as yourself: I am the LORD," follows a verse that gives one example of how to love the neighbor, "You shall not hate in your heart anyone of your kin; you shall reprove your neighbor, or you will incur guilt yourself" (Leviticus 19:17). To "reprove" is to "rebuke." Dismas is trying to call Gestas into responsibility and repentance. He is, ironically again, being a good neighbor.

The Lucan phrase, "the other rebuked him," does not use the same Greek word for "rebuke" as that found in the Septuagint (the early Greek translation of the Hebrew text) of Leviticus 19:17. However, the word that the good thief uses does appear elsewhere in Luke's Gospel; in many cases, Jesus uses the term to rebuke—connoting both to silence and to disempower—in the context of dealing with the demonic. In Luke 4:35; 4:41; 9:42 Jesus "rebukes" demons during an exorcism; in 4:39 he rebukes the fever from which Peter's mother-in-law suffers and thereby heals her (we can think of the fever as a demon; I suspect anyone who has had a hot flash will understand the connection easily), and so on. Yet in Luke's Gospel, Jesus also states, "Be on your guard! If your brother sins, you must rebuke the offender, and if there is repentance, you must forgive" (Luke 17:3).

We can thus read the second victim's comment in one of two ways. Either he is treating his fellow victim like a demon, like a fever, like a cyclone, or he is issuing an invitation to repentance. I prefer the second reading, since neither of these two men is a demon, or an illness, or a force of nature. Both are human beings, and both, sentenced to death, are dying.

*"Do you not fear God, since you are under the same sentence of condemnation? And we indeed have been condemned justly, for we are getting what we deserve for our deeds" (Luke 23:40b-41a).*

The concern for fearing God takes on heightened implications: all three men dying on crosses have been judged by human courts, but the only judge to fear—the only judge who has the true power of eternal life versus oblivion—is the God to whom Jesus prays, "Father, forgive them." We readers of Luke have heard people speak of fearing God before. In the first chapter, Zechariah, the father of John the Baptizer, exclaimed, "His mercy is for those who fear him / from generation to generation" (Luke 1:50). The mercy the good thief did not find from the ancient equivalent of the criminal justice system he will instead find with God.

While Dismas, who also comes into history as the "penitent thief," does not explicitly state he repents from his evildoing, at least he acknowledges it. He does not deny, and he does not excuse. Thus, he provides a lesson in how we can and should take responsibility for our own actions, major or minor, that would run counter to morality. Rather than, "Well, yes, I did...run the stop sign, take the jewelry without paying for it, cheat a bit on the taxes..." all the way to "I was too busy to take the time to visit..." or whatever excuses we make, sometimes the better move is to admit, "I was wrong."

My insider students approve the man's admitting to the charge. They take issue, as do I, with the comment "We are getting what we deserve" (the Greek has the connotation of "worth" or a just repayment). No one deserves to be tortured to death. Thus, the dying man's words force questions of justice: What is the penalty to be paid by the secretary who pilfers from the company, the member of the clergy who abuses a congregant, the contractor who skimps on materials and builds a condominium that collapses?

For some of my students, divine justice is so offended by our sins, whether major or minor, that we can never be punished to the extent we deserve. Therefore, Jesus had to die. I prefer to think of God as a forgiving parent, who insists we take responsibility for our actions but who is also ready to forgive us. The story of divine mercy and divine justice will always be told in different ways.

### Then he said, "Jesus, remember me when you come into your kingdom" (Luke 23:42).

There's a text-critical problem with this verse, which means that ancient manuscripts have different readings. We've seen a similar problem with that pesky verse Mark 15:28. The NRSV reads "come *into* your kingdom" (emphasis added). Other ancient Greek manuscripts read "come *in* your kingdom." Prepositions do matter. The first reading, "Come into your kingdom," implies that *in the present*, and thus in heaven, Jesus will welcome him. The second, "come in your kingdom," suggests that the man will have a place among the risen disciples when Jesus returns "in his glory and the glory of the Father and of the holy angels" (Luke 9:26b).

Before we get to the "where and when" of the kingdom, we need to take time for the "what" of being remembered. My insider students want to be remembered. After my first semester at Riverbend, one of the insiders asked me if I would come back and teach another class. I assured him I would. He smiled and said something to the effect of "That's what you all say." Another simply asked, "Please remember me." I kept my promise to return, and I continue to remember them.

The call to remember is not just a plea for an afterlife marked by freedom rather than imprisonment; a call to remember is to make sure we do not treat our fellow human beings like numbers on a uniform or at a roll call, but that we treat them as individuals. A call to remember is to think about justice, in sentencing, in how prisons house and feed individuals, in what the justice system can do to help in rehabilitation, in attending to the concerns of the victims and their families, and also to the families of perpetrators.

Next, a call to remember is to evoke the numerous commandments that begin with exhortations to remember, because memory can provoke ethical responses. "Remember that you were a slave in the land of Egypt; therefore I am commanding you to do this" (Deuteronomy 24:22). To create a new kingdom requires knowing our history and how it affects us in the present. Indeed, if we don't learn our histories then we cannot remember them, and if we do not remember them, we cannot learn from them.

Memory is especially important in cases of death, and all three men are dying. They force the question of memory back to us. Whether we are mostly saint or mostly sinner (we're all a combination of both), we may wonder, "How will I be remembered?" or even "Who will remember me?" We see in the Beatitude, "Blessed are those who mourn, for they will be comforted" (Matthew 5:4), and we know that memory can be important in the mourning process. Here, at the cross, in Luke, the subject shifts. This dying man knows that the cross is not the end of the story. For Jesus to "remember" him, Jesus must have a mind and a heart that can remember. The end therefore cannot be, for Jesus, oblivion.

We tend to think of remembering those who have died, so that we are the ones doing the remembering. Luke allows us a different view: What would it mean to think about those who have died *remembering us?*

Or, to put the question in theological language: What might it mean to know that *God remembers us*, that we are not forgotten, that we matter? The first time the term *remember* occurs in the Bible, it bespeaks a divine memory of all humanity. Following the flood, God promises: "I will remember my covenant that is between me and you and every living creature of all flesh; and the waters shall never again become a flood to destroy all flesh" (Genesis 9:15). In the Hebrew Bible, the term for *memory* in its various forms appears 213 times, often in terms of God remembering the covenants made with humanity. Memory works both ways.

While we do not have this man's name—he comes into reception history as Dismas—he knows Jesus's name. "Jesus..." he says. He is the only person in the Gospel to call Jesus simply by his name (this is a good trivia question, in case you're collecting them). Not "lord" or "rabbi" or "teacher" or "Son of God," he addresses Jesus by name. In Luke's Gospel, people call Jesus by his name only in times of extreme difficulty. Ten men suffering from leprosy call out to him, "Jesus, Master, have mercy on us" (Luke 17:13). A blind beggar shouts, "Jesus, Son of David, have mercy on me!" (Luke 18:38). Demons, about to be exorcised, identity him as "Jesus of Nazareth...the Holy One of God" (Luke 4:34) and as "Jesus, Son of the Most High God" (Luke 8:28). Now we have, simply, "Jesus."

The name *Jesus* is an Anglicized version of the Greek *Iesous*, which is a Greek rendition of the Aramaic *Yeshu* or *Yeshua*, which comes from the Hebrew root meaning "salvation" (cognates include *hosanna* as well as the names Hosea and Joshua). Saying the name *Jesus* thus is a plea for salvation. But the name is also an intimate address. Jesus—and both other victims in Mark—knows exactly what the other men are feeling, in his aching shoulders, his gasping lungs. No need for titles; no strength to speak. The dying man addresses Jesus by name. No need for titles, no need to include a doxology. Their suffering binds them together rather than alienates them.

The dying evildoer admits his guilt, rebukes his neighbor, defends Jesus, and calls Jesus by his name. He does even more. Jesus had been speaking of the "kingdom of God," and the titulus on the cross reads "King of the Jews." The dying man understands what this kingdom is. "When you come into your kingdom," he states. Golgotha, the place of the skull, is *not* the kingdom. It is the opposite of the kingdom.

Now we can return to that text-critical problem of "come into" versus "come in" the kingdom. Several times, Luke couples references to the "kingdom of God" with the notice that Jesus healed the sick. For example, Luke 9:11b describes how Jesus spoke to the crowd about the "kingdom of God, and healed those who needed to be cured." The dying man knew of this reputation. He knows that Jesus can heal bodies, and he sees Jesus's own body, scourged, bloodied, nailed, outstretched. He knows that Jesus has raised the dead, and now he sees Jesus dying. One man sees Jesus and derides him; the other sees and, astonishingly, sees past the torture and the death to new life.

His "remember me" is both a plea and a demand. His reference to a kingdom into which Jesus will enter shows the difference between the Roman Empire and the realm of God. In two verses, a dying man, gasping for breath, has made the perfect prayer. As for the distinction of now or later, Jesus changes the question.

### He replied, "Truly I tell you, today you will be with me in Paradise" (Luke 23:43).

Is the kingdom now or later? Jesus changes the terms of the request. Jesus's response continues to engage historians and theologians. Some of my students have questioned how the fellow can enter paradise without having been baptized. Personally, I doubt Jesus was worried about that. Others wonder about the change to the man's request. The man had spoken about Jesus's kingdom. Jesus responds by speaking not about the kingdom, but about *paradise* (that is the Greek term). His response offers the man even more than he had asked.

Beneath the "Truly" of the English translation lies the term *"amen."* To the man's prayer, Jesus offers the response: "Amen, so be it." And then he does more. The man spoke of Jesus's kingdom, whether taking place on earth already or when he returns in glory, when the kingdom of God will be fully established. Jesus speaks of the comfort to the man *now*.

We have another text-critical problem here, this one a matter not of prepositions but of punctuation. Either Jesus stated, "Amen, I tell you today, you will be with me in Paradise" (i.e., today, at this moment, I am telling you what will happen later) or "Amen, I tell you, today you will be with me in Paradise" (i.e., today, this very day, you will be with me in Paradise). Commas make all the difference. While there are a number of theologians who prefer the first option and thus a delay, I find the second more consistent with Luke's Gospel and Acts.

"Today," Jesus says; not years, or decades, or centuries from now, but today. Today, the man will be released from his suffering; today he will be forgiven his sins; today he will be in paradise where the righteous dwell. Jesus had already given a glimpse of this setting in the parable of the rich man and Lazarus (Luke 16:19-31), where the suffering Lazarus rests in the (proverbial) bosom of Abraham (16:23; most English translations resist this literal reading; perhaps *bosom* was too difficult a term). Similarly, Paul speaks of being "caught up into Paradise" (2 Corinthians 12:4). The kingdom will come in the future, but paradise already exists in the present.

In the Book of Acts, Peter assures his Jerusalem audience that "Jesus...must remain in heaven until the time of universal restoration" (3:21). Dismas will be in paradise now and, at that universal restoration, will enter into the kingdom.

Even more, the promise of paradise is not, at least as I read the verse, the main point. The greater import is the simple word, *me*. "Remember *me*," the supplicant asks. Jesus responds, "You will be with *me*." In his Epistle to the Philippians, Paul—who is in prison under a death sentence—writes, "If I am to live in the flesh, that means fruitful labor for me; and I do not know which I prefer. I am hard pressed between the two: my desire is to depart and be with Christ, for that is far better" (Philippians 1:22-23). We might think of paradise as the garden of Eden or the bosom of Abraham, where everything is perfect. But the place may be less important than the company we keep. We might shift our concern from *where* we shall live to *with whom* we shall live.

The penitent victim is "with Jesus" all along, in dying and in paradise. They have each other. Luke gives no indication that either of the two other victims had friends or family at the cross; in Luke's Gospel, "all [of Jesus's] acquaintances, including the women who had followed him from Galilee, stood at a distance, watching these things" (Luke 23:49). They are with him in spirit, but only Dismas is with him in body, with him close enough to talk, with him close enough to pray.

When we feel forsaken by God, and we all will at one point or another, will we have such a friend who will "remember me"? More, can we be this friend?

## And now?

The stories of these men continue. Early commentators speculated on their crimes, with some opting for robbing and murder (here with echoes of the robbers on that road to Jericho where the

Samaritan of the parable aids the wounded man); some opting for fratricide and so evoking the story of Cain and Abel. I wonder if it matters. For what crimes would we want people executed? What background stories, or "mitigating circumstances," would make a difference in the sentencing?

The supporting and supplicating thief enters the realm of Christian legend, through the fourth-century apocryphal Gospel of Nicodemus, where he receives the name Dismas; later traditions give him additional names. While anonymous characters, like the Beloved Disciple, the other women at the cross, and the centurion whom we meet in the next chapter, play major roles, naming—and especially the naming of these two men who die with Jesus—may be a good start in helping us to remember not just other victims of violence but also other people executed.

Finally, a moment of discomfort: we do not know what exactly these men did, other than works of evil. We do not know who their victims were, what they lost, or what they suffered. In working at Riverbend, I am reminded always not only of my friendship with my insider students but also of their victims. I do not ask the men what they did, and only in one case did I go to the internet to see if rumors were true (they were). But many of them tell me, whether in papers or in class discussion. What is my responsibility to the victims? And what would their victims think of these two men, dying on that hill so many years ago?

# Chapter 3

# THE SOLDIERS

The Gospel of Mark records the presence of a Roman military detachment on Golgotha: Roman hands crucify Jesus, and Roman eyes watch him die. At the foot of the cross, Roman soldiers cast dice for Jesus's garments; on the cross, Jesus dies, not only alone but also naked. Then something astonishing happens. "Now when the centurion, who stood facing him, saw that in this way he breathed his last, he said, 'Truly this man was God's Son'" (Mark 15:39).

It's possible this army officer was being facetious: This dead Jew—this scourged, contorted, naked Jew—this fellow is the one people call a son of God? Ridiculous. But even if he were facetious, he ironically makes the correct confession. Such a reading is consistent with how the narrative functions. Pilate is facetious in having the charge against Jesus read "King of the Jews." Pilate had no idea how true that title was, but Mark's readers do.

The centurion has one more role to play. According to Mark 15:44, "Then Pilate wondered if [Jesus] were already dead," and so "summoning the centurion, he asked him whether [Jesus] had been dead for some time." Victims of crucifixion could suffer that torture not just for three hours but, often, for days. The centurion offers his testimony, his witness, to Pilate that Jesus had died. When Pilate "learned from the centurion that he was dead, he granted the body to Joseph" (Mark 15:45). The centurion thus bears witness that Jesus was dead. Jesus had not fainted, only to be find himself awake later. He had not been given a drug to make him appear dead, only to rise when the drug wore off. He was dead. The centurion, the military officer, would recognize death.

The author of Matthew's Gospel, perhaps seeking to assure readers that the centurion was not being facetious, adds details to explain how he came to his conclusion: "Now when the centurion and those with him, who were keeping watch over Jesus, saw the earthquake and what took place, they were terrified and said, 'Truly this man was God's Son!'"(Matthew 27:54). Just as Matthew offers the heavenly portent of the Star of Bethlehem at Jesus's birth, so Matthew offers natural wonders to accompany Jesus at his death. Just as Matthew depicts the Gentile magi as recognizing Jesus's kingly status (those high-end birthday gifts), so Matthew depicts a Gentile at the cross as recognizing Jesus's divine status

A third variant of the account appears in Luke's Gospel. Here the centurion is cast as a believer in the God of Israel; perhaps we are to see him as a God-fearer, a Gentile who affiliated with Jews but did not convert to Judaism. This officer "praised God and said [according to the NRSV translation], 'Certainly this man was innocent'" (Luke 23:47). In the original Greek of the New Testament, however, the centurion pronounces Jesus not "innocent" but "righteous" (Greek: *dikaios*).

There is no centurion mentioned explicitly in the Fourth Gospel. To the contrary, John 4:46-54 offers a variant of a story Matthew (8:5-13) and Luke (7:1-10) tell about a centurion living in Capernaum whose slave (or son; the Greek for Matthew is ambiguous) Jesus heals. In John's version, the petitioner is not a centurion, an army officer, but a "royal official," perhaps one connected to Herod Antipas; in John's version, Luke's "slave" becomes the official's son. It may be that John wants to avoid connecting Jesus to high-ranking soldiers. Seeing how the Evangelists depict the Roman military presence can help us ask the right questions about the military stationed outside their homelands today: Do they understand the people among whom they live? Do they treat them with respect? Do they bother to learn the local language?

Concerning the witnesses at the cross, the Fourth Gospel elaborates on the details the Synoptics provide. For example, Mark notes that the soldiers "divided his clothes among them, casting lots to decide what each should take" (Mark 15:24, see also Matthew 27:35; Luke 23:34b). The verse alludes to Psalm 22:18, "They divide my clothes among themselves, / and for my clothing they cast lots." Mark and Matthew do not tell us this is an allusion, but given the role of Psalm 22 from the cry of dereliction onward, the Gospels anticipate that we readers will make the connection.

The Fourth Evangelist, perhaps having encountered a reader or two of the other Gospels who did not get the connection, turns the details into a fulfillment citation:

> *When the soldiers had crucified Jesus, they took his clothes and divided them into four parts, one for each soldier. They also took his tunic; now the tunic was seamless, woven in one piece from the top. So they said to one another, "Let us not tear it, but cast lots for it to see who will get it." This was to fulfill what the scripture says,*
>
> > *"They divided my clothes among themselves,*
> > *and for my clothing they cast lots."*
> > *John 19:23-24*

The citation is a direct quotation of the Greek (Septuagint) translation of Psalm 22:18. Whereas the psalm is written in poetic parallelism, so that "They divide my clothes among themselves" and "for my clothing they cast lots" are two ways of expressing the same point, John separates the two halves of the verse and depicts the events at the cross as fulfilling both of them. The "clothes" in the first half of the verse are what the soldiers divide and apportion among themselves; the "clothing" (singular) in the second half of the verse becomes in John's text a "seamless garment." Afficionados of classic movies may recall the 1953 epic, *The Robe*, starring Richard Burton, Jean Simmons, and Victor Mature, based on Lloyd C. Douglas's novel. The robe itself, the seamless garment, continues to feature in the equally fabulous 1954 sequel, *Demetrius and the Gladiators*.

John also adds detail to support the centurion's report to Pilate concerning Jesus's death. To understand these details, it helps to know that the Fourth Gospel dates Jesus's death not to the first day of Passover (therefore, in John's Gospel, the Last Supper is not a seder, a Passover meal) but to the day before, at the time the lambs for the Paschal offering are being sacrificed in the Jerusalem Temple. John 19:31 gives both the calendrical detail and its implication. The verse begins, "Since it was the day of Preparation," that is, the day the lambs are sacrificed. Jewish families, on pilgrimage to Jerusalem, would that evening celebrate the Passover by eating the lambs they obtained from the Temple together with bitter herbs and unleavened bread and by telling the story of the Exodus from Egypt.

John continues, "The Jews did not want the bodies left on the cross during the sabbath, especially because that sabbath was a day of great solemnity" (John 19:31). One cannot celebrate the Sabbath, the day of rest, let alone Passover, the feast of freedom from slavery in Egypt, and at the same time allow bodies executed by the state to go unburied. John may also be alluding here to Deuteronomy 21:22-23, "When someone is convicted of a crime punishable by death and is executed, and you hang him on a tree, his corpse must not remain all night upon the tree; you shall bury him that same day, for anyone hung on a tree is under God's curse. You must not defile the land that the LORD your God is giving you for possession." Paul gives a new interpretation of this verse in Galatians 3:13 to talk about salvation: "Christ redeemed us from the curse of the law by becoming a curse for us—for it is written, 'Cursed is everyone who hangs on a tree.'"

Deuteronomy, by the way, is not talking about someone executed by hanging or impaling. The victim is stoned, and then the body is temporarily displayed as a warning to others. The Greek (Septuagint) reading of Deuteronomy suggests that the body is cursed by God, and that reading underlies Paul's exegesis. The Hebrew, however, suggests that the person is not cursed by God, but cursed "of God." One rabbinic interpretation suggests that God feels cursed with the execution of an individual, since all people are in the divine image and likeness. The NRSV, as we've seen, reads, "anyone hung on a tree is under God's curse." The Jewish Publication Society translation has "For an impaled body is an affront to God."

Given their concern to remove the body before sunset, the Jews "asked Pilate to have the legs of the crucified men broken and the bodies removed" (John 19:31). The request, which sounds grisly to modern ears, was a plea for the mercy to hasten death. Victims of crucifixion usually died by asphyxiation since they could not get enough air into their lungs. Broken legs would mean that the victims could no longer push up their bodies and so fill their lungs.

"The soldiers came and broke the legs of the first and of the other who had been crucified with him. But when they came to Jesus and saw that he was already dead, they did not break his legs. Instead, one of the soldiers pierced his side with a spear, and at once blood and water came out" (John 19:32-34). Again, John tells us that the events fulfilled Scripture. The first notice is "These things occurred so that the scripture might be fulfilled, 'None of his bones shall be broken'" (John 19:36); the text alludes to both Exodus 12:46, the commandment that "you shall not break any of [the Paschal offering's] bones," and Psalm 34:19-20, which concerns the "afflictions of the righteous," that "the LORD rescues them. . . . / He keeps all their bones; / not one of them will be broken."

The Gospel text then adds, "And again another passage of scripture says, 'They will look on the one whom they have pierced'" (John 19:37). The allusion, but not a direct citation to either the Hebrew or the Greek, is to Zechariah 12:10, which the NRSV translates as "And I will pour out a spirit of compassion and supplication on the house of David and the inhabitants of Jerusalem, so that, when they look on the one whom they have pierced, they shall mourn for him, as one mourns for an only child, and weep bitterly over him, as one weeps over a firstborn." The Hebrew underlying this final citation is itself unclear, for the "pierced" may refer to either an individual or to a group. If we read Zechariah 12:10 in light of the previous verse, "And on that day I will seek to destroy all the nations that come against Jerusalem" (Zechariah 12:9), then the "pierced" should refer to one of the nations.

A side note: In the Jewish tradition, Zechariah 12:10 comes to have messianic implications, but not about Jesus. The Babylonian Talmud (b. Sukkah 52a) suggests it refers to the Messiah ben Joseph, the Messiah representing the northern tribes of Israel, who dies in the eschatological battle. After this, the Messiah ben David brings about divine justice. Another reading is that the one killed is the "evil inclination."

These different depictions invite readers to raise new sets of questions and, in developing answers, find new understandings not only of the death of Jesus but also of the soldiers and of how we understand prophecy. In this chapter, we'll see how Matthew 8:5-13 and Luke 7:1-10 foreshadow the role of the centurion at the cross by depicting Jesus interacting with a centurion in Galilee, how the centurion at the cross anticipates Cornelius, the first Roman to join the movement gathered in Jesus's name (Acts 10), the implications of the title "Son of God," and the reasons why Luke might have shifted the pronouncement to one of Jesus as "righteous" or "innocent."

At the end, we'll see what one Roman officer—both responsible for the death of Jesus under horrendous torture and responding in faith to his death—teaches us about our actions in the past and how, in light of our recognitions of responsibility, we can live more faithfully and compassionately into the future.

## Who Were the Centurions?

I recall, as a child, being confused by the terms "centaur" and "centurion." I knew from books on Greek mythology, which I devoured, that centaurs were half-human (always men) and half-horse, that they were great at archery, and that they were very wise. Then I read the Narnia books by C. S. Lewis and again found centaurs, who were faithful to the dying-rising lion Aslan. (I had no clue that Lewis was writing about Christianity!) I learned about centurions first from my early years of listening to Gospel stories and seeing pictures of Gospel narratives: in depictions of Jesus's crucifixion, often present at the cross were soldiers, whether playing dice, or a soldier piercing Jesus's side with a spear, or a soldier looking up at Jesus with amazement or guilt or both. There were also centurions in the old movies I'd watch on television, although as I realize now, at the time neither I nor the movies were all that old: not only *The Robe* and *Demetrius and the Gladiators* but also *Quo Vadis* (1951), *Ben Hur* (1959), *Spartacus* (1960), and a host of other "sword and sandal" epics. Centurions and centaurs—generally wise, trustworthy, and great to have on your side in a fight.

Centurions are Roman army officers, some who rose through the ranks rather than received a commission via patronage or familial connections. The name comes into Latin from the Greek *hekatontarchos*, literally "ruler/leader" (*archon*) "of 100" (*hekaton*); the centurion headed a "century," which should have been a unit of one hundred soldiers but in fact consisted of eighty legionaries. In describing the Roman military, the second-century BCE Greek historian Polybius (*History* book VI) states that centurions— elected by the tribunes—are expected to be natural leaders, not headstrong but steady, not inclined to attack but ready to protect their posts at all costs. After Rome shifted in governance from being a republic to being an empire (i.e., ruled by an emperor, starting with Julius Caesar), emperors could and did appoint centurions. These officers were usually literate, the pay was relatively good, a number gained Roman citizenship, and the work included both administrative and judicial roles. To put this in modern terms, the centurion is someone for whom you would quickly accept when a friend set you up on a date.

At the time of Jesus, there were no Roman soldiers stationed in Galilee. The centurion in Capernaum (Matthew 8:5; Luke 7:1), which is in Galilee, may have been a member of one of Herod Antipas's auxiliary forces, usually compromised of Syrians. In Judea, which is where Jerusalem is located, Pontius Pilate had his own troops. However, it was only after the destruction of the Temple in 70 CE that Rome stationed a legion (the 10th, called *Fratensis*) in Judea. Acts 10:1 identifies Cornelius as "a centurion of the Italian Cohort" and Acts 27:1 mentions that Paul was transferred into the custody of "a centurion of the Augustan Cohort, named Julius." This cohort was based in Syria.

The centurion at the cross is not the only Roman military figure the New Testament mentions. We've already met the soldiers in Luke's Gospel, to whom the Baptizer instructs, "Do not extort money from anyone by threats or false accusation, and be satisfied with your wages" (Luke 3:14). Following the Sermon on the Mount, in which Jesus exhorts his disciples, "If someone strikes you on the right cheek, turn the other also" (Matthew 5:39) and "If anyone forces you to go one mile, go also the second mile" (5:41), Jesus encounters the centurion of Matthew 8:5-13. Since Roman army officers would be prime candidates for giving locals in the colonies a backhanded slap or, as we saw with Simon of Cyrene, conscripting locals to do the heavy lifting, the juxtaposition of the Sermon on the Mount and the centurion attends to how the followers of Jesus, anywhere in the Roman Empire (and subsequently), should react to governmental officials with military connections.

The Gospels also use other Roman military titles. Mark 5:9 (cf. Luke 8:30) depicts Jesus's encounter with a demon-possessed man who self-identifies, "My name is Legion; for we are many" (Matthew's Gospel drops the name of the demons). A legion is an army unit comprised of between 5,500 and 6,000 men, so readers get the message that being possessed by demons is comparable to being occupied by an invading army. For a different type of legion, at his arrest, Jesus says to the crowd that had come to arrest him in Gethsemane, "Do you think that I cannot appeal to my Father, and he will at once send me more than twelve legions of angels?" (Matthew 26:53). Those angelic legions are the so-called "heavenly host."

The basic parameters of the Roman army system would have been as familiar to Jesus and his followers, and to the audiences of the Gospels, as we are today with terms like "admiral" or "general" or "lieutenant." We may not all know the respective ranks and job descriptions, but when we hear "general" we know we are speaking of someone with more authority than "private" or "sergeant." And when we hear comments like "soldiers of Christ" or sing "Onward Christian Soldiers," we import some of these ideas as well.

## The Centurion of Matthew 8:5-13 and Luke 7:2-10

After the Sermon on the Mount, Jesus begins a series of healings. He first restores a man suffering from leprosy (likely a type of skin disease and not Hansen's disease) by "cleansing" him and thus restoring him to ritual purity. Jesus, to show his continuing fidelity not only to the Torah but also to the Temple, then commands the man to show himself to the priest and to offer the sacrifice (not to worry, the Temple worked on a sliding scale, so money for the offering was not a problem) offered for such healing.

Next, entering Capernaum (*caper* is the Greek version of the Aramaic *k'far*, meaning "town," and *naum* is the name Nahum, so the place could be called Nahumsville), Jesus is approached by a centurion, an officer. The centurion makes an indirect request in the form of a declarative statement, which was considered the polite way of asking. Rather than asking, "Will you please heal my servant (or slave)?" he states, "Lord (Greek: *kyrios*), my servant (Greek *pais*, which can also mean "child") is lying at home paralyzed" (Matthew 8:6). We find a similar approach at the wedding at Cana, when Jesus's mother tells him, "They have no wine" (John 2:3). I have been known to engage in this same type of expression. "Your homework is not done" is less an observation than it is a request if not an order.

The centurion is not simply conveying information; he wants Jesus to perform the healing. His addressing Jesus as *kyrios* can have the connotation of "sir" (as in "lords and ladies"), but it is also the Greek term used to translate the Hebrew name of God, YHWH. Matthew leaves it up to the readers to determine what inflection we want to give the term. At the same time, we might pause to think what it means to call Jesus "Lord." Do we think "social superior" or do we think "divine Savior"?

Scholars debate the tenor of Jesus's response, since biblical Greek has no punctuation marks. Either Jesus responded with an emphatic "I will come and cure him!" (Matthew 8:7) or he responded with a question, "Shall I come and cure him?" The centurion's response fits either reading, although I admit I am partial to the question: in Matthew's Gospel, Jesus initially restricts his messianic activities to his fellow Jews. This Gentile centurion has, to use an athletic rather than a military image, jumped the gun. He thus anticipates the Gentile mission.

The centurion then asserts both his own humility in relation to Jesus and his conviction that Jesus can perform the healing: "Lord, I am not worthy to have you come under my roof, but only speak the word, and my servant will be healed" (Matthew 8:8). The comments are, like the statement of the centurion at the cross, astonishing. A senior military officer recognizes that this Jew from Nazareth has more authority than he!

The centurion continues: "For I also am a man under authority, with soldiers under me; and I say to one, 'Go,' and he goes, and to another, 'Come,' and he comes, and to my slave, 'Do this,' and the slave does it" (Matthew 8:9). We readers will recognize the full import of this statement after we have read the entire Gospel and then returned to the beginning. First, the centurion is speaking of not only the obedience but also the trust that marks the Roman military system. Just as the centurion needs to be able to trust the tribunes above him, so his legionnaires need to be able to trust him. That trust is how members of the assembly gathered in Jesus's name are to function. Second, while the centurion notes the role of the enslaved, his next step is to recognize his own status as enslaved, with only God (and not the emperor) as his master. To read his statement and not to notice the role of the enslaved would be to ignore the ongoing legacy of slavery rather than to address it. Next, Jesus will later tell his disciples that they must act as if they were enslaved (e.g., Matthew 20:27, "Whoever wishes to be first among you must be your slave.") Finally, Jesus himself takes on the role of one enslaved, and, as the Gospels indicate, he goes to the cross as God wants, in obedience to the divine will and not to his own (Matthew 26:42).

The centurion is coming close to knowing how the enslaved feel: that they are under orders, that they are not free to follow their own will. To begin to understand what it means to be a slave is to begin both to recognize the ongoing legacy of slavery and to begin to find ways of addressing it. Jesus recognizes this centurion's extraordinary statement. "He was amazed and said to those who followed him, 'Truly I tell you, in no one in Israel have I found such faith'" (Matthew 8:10). He then offers a prediction of "many" coming "from east and west" to "eat with Abraham, Isaac, and Jacob in the kingdom of heaven" (Matthew 8:11). While the original statement may have referred to the return to the land of Israel of Jews in the Diaspora, in the context of Matthew's Gospel, the statement refers to foreigners, Gentiles, who will participate with the patriarchs in the messianic banquet.

Before Jesus pronounces the good news that the servant has been healed, he makes one final comment. While the centurion and those like him will dine at the messianic banquet, "the heirs of the kingdom will be thrown into the outer darkness, where there will be weeping and gnashing of teeth" (Matthew 8:12). The scene, we only learn later, anticipates the witnesses at the cross. The Gentile centurion makes the right proclamation, while, as we have seen, "the chief priests, along with the scribes, were also mocking him among themselves and saying, 'He saved others; he cannot save himself'" (Mark 15:31).

Luke 7:2-10 tells the same story, more or less. In Luke's version, we never meet the centurion. Instead, the centurion sends Jewish elders to plead with Jesus on his behalf, for his slave (Greek: *doulos*) is ill. The elders explain that the centurion is a God-fearer: "He is worthy of having you do this for him," they state, and then they give the reasons: "He loves our people, and it is he who built our synagogue for us" (Luke 7:3-5). As Jesus heads to heal the slave, the centurion sends another set of messengers to convey the points we saw in Matthew 8 concerning his humility, conviction that Jesus can heal from a distance, and his place in the chain of command. Jesus again expresses his amazement that a Gentile would make such a confession. Amazed that a *Gentile*, a *Gentile soldier*, would make such a confession? Just wait.

## The Difficult Readings

Before we leave our centurion, two more points about how he is understood in reception history. These are difficult issues, but they are also issues with which the biblical text can be of help. The Bible, I have often said, is a book that helps us ask the right questions. It does not always provide answers, but by encouraging those who hold it sacred to speak to each other about difficult matters, it may lead us in good directions.

First, some readers see the ailing individual as a slave whose paralysis stems from the trauma of being owned by a Roman officer; they take his ailment as a psychosomatic reaction to having his mind and body abused. Thus, they suggest that the reason the centurion does not want Jesus to come to his home is because he doesn't want Jesus to see their intimate and therefore abusive living arrangements. While I understand this reading, I do not find it helpful. It sets up Jesus as complicit in a system of abuse. I choose to read the ailing individual as exactly that, one who is physically suffering and one who finds an unlikely advocate in the Roman officer.

Second, other readers compare the paralysis to the ailments of the Gerasene man who identified himself as "Legion" and so again see the despair and destruction that armies can create in the lands and among the people they conquer. Again, while I understand this reading, and I do agree that the name "Legion" for the host of demons is an anti-Roman jibe, I do not see the centurion as in the Gospel narrative as a negative character. And yet. He represents an occupation. To see him as a positive figure threatens to ignore the brutal power of the Roman Empire. To see him as a negative figure threatens to ignore, especially, the figure in Luke who "loves our nation and built for us our synagogue." How do we assess such a figure? Again, the Bible helps us ask the right questions, even as it opens to multiple answers.

I doubt that this centurion in Capernaum is the same centurion who appears at the foot of the cross. There is no reason for a man stationed in, or having retired to, Capernaum to find himself among Pilate's troops in Judea. Yet I see this first centurion in Matthew 8/Luke 7 as anticipating the man at the cross and then, later, both Cornelius in Caesarea in Acts 10 and the centurion who helps Paul on the way to Rome at the end of Acts. Each figure is an individual, but none can be fully divorced from the others. We always carry both our individuality and the legacy, for better or worse, of others in our community.

## The Centurion at the Cross

We can now more fully appreciate the centurion at the cross. I imagine him to be a man of intelligence, literate, politically savvy, probably not happy with being on execution detail (I do wonder if the soldiers who executed Jesus were not officers, which is what

John's Gospel suggests; perhaps Mark, followed by Matthew and Luke, gave one an upgrade to enhance the importance of Jesus's death). Perhaps he was even interested in Jews and Judaism. We do not know if he had heard of Jesus, but he did read the titulus, the inscription on the cross (more often it was hung around the neck of the victim), "King of the Jews" (Matthew 27:37; Mark 15:26; Luke 23:38; cf. John 19:19, 21-22). Perhaps he pitied Jesus; perhaps he thought, "This is what happens when you gain a following in Jerusalem at a festival"; perhaps he was sympathetic to the Jews who chafed under Roman domination.

Watching Jesus die, he states, according to Mark's Greek text, "Truly, this man a son of God was" (Mark 15:39). The NRSV offers the more mellifluous "Truly this man was God's Son!" but the footnote offers the more accurate alternative, "*a son of God*." We can understand this statement in multiple ways.

The first, as we've seen, is that the centurion is being facetious. This fellow, this naked, dead, crowned-with-thorns fellow, is a son of God? This fellow is comparable to the emperor? This fellow? For Mark's Gospel is, "Yes, THIS fellow, who dies as a 'ransom for many'" (Mark 10:45). The centurion in this reading does not realize the truth of his own statement. In reception history, he will become not a doubter but a believer.

A second reading sees the centurion as making a statement based in pagan belief: he sees Jesus not as *the* Son of God but as *a* son of God, the child of a divine parent and a human one. In this reading, Jesus is comparable to Dionysus (also called Bacchus, as in Sophocles's play, *The Bacchae*), who both died and who had an afterlife among the gods. Jesus's connections with wine drinking (e.g., his comment, "The Son of Man came eating and drinking, and they say, 'Look, a glutton and a drunkard, a friend of tax collectors and sinners!'" [Matthew 11:19]), turning water into wine (John 2:1–10), his self-identification, "I am the true vine and my Father is the vinegrower" (John 15:1), his having women followers, and the eating of divine flesh suggested in the Eucharistic celebrations all commend the Dionysian connections. The centurion thus becomes someone on the way to recognizing Jesus's true role, but he's not there yet.

A third reading, sensitive to Mark's Christology, affirms what the Gospel has been saying all along: Jesus's primary role is not to be seen in the miracles. Jesus, with some consistency, tells people he healed to be quiet about the mighty work done for them. Nor is his role primarily in the teachings, which tend to come in parables; Mark has no Sermon on the Mount (so Matthew) or Sermon on the Plain (so Luke). Rather, only after Peter identifies Jesus as the Messiah does Jesus tell the disciples about his mission: "Then he began to teach them that the Son of Man must undergo great suffering, and be rejected by the elders, the chief priests, and the scribes, and be killed, and after three days rise again. He said all this quite openly" (Mark 8:31-32a). This is the first of three passion predictions. To focus on the miracles is to miss the point. The centurion, focusing on the cross, gets the point. The disciples, unable to accept this teaching, are nowhere to be found.

In Luke's rewrite, the centurion does not refer to Jesus as a son of God. For Luke, *all* people are children of God. Luke's version of the genealogy begins with Jesus, and it traces his line back through King David, and through Abraham, all the way to "son of Enos, son of Seth, son of Adam, son of God" (Luke 3:38). Moreover, Luke has already indicated that Jesus will be called "Son of God," for example, in Gabriel's annunciation to Mary (Luke 1:35). The devil challenges Jesus to claim the title (4:3, 9) and the demons name Jesus "Son of God" (4:41). When at his trial the priests ask, "Are you, then, the Son of God?" he responds, "You say that I am" 22:70). The evangelist knows this will become the preferred title for Jesus, but that is not the title needed at the cross. The centurion, the representative of Rome's army and therefore the representative of another form of leadership, has a different role to play.

When Luke's centurion "saw what had taken place, he praised God and said, 'Certainly this man was innocent'" (23:47). First, what did he see? He read the titulus and heard the taunting. He heard Jesus pray, "Father, forgive them; for they do not know what they are doing" (23:34). Only in Luke's Gospel does Jesus offer this prayer, which comes immediately after the description of where the soldiers crucified Jesus and immediately before the announcement that they played dice for his clothing. Thus, Jesus's prayer refers to the soldiers. Was the centurion, amazed at this expression of generosity, acknowledging that Jesus was righteous?

The centurion also saw one of the other victims defending Jesus and recognizing his kingship, and he saw other people, including the "daughters of Jerusalem" whom we meet two chapters hence, bearing witness in sympathy and in mourning. He heard Jesus assure a dying man, "Today you will be with me in Paradise." Would any of this be enough to convince the centurion that Jesus was innocent?

Or was he convinced by the heavenly portents, "It was now about noon, and darkness came over the whole land until three in the afternoon" (23:44)? Or, again, was he convinced by Jesus's affirmation of his relationship to God, for right before the centurion's confession, Jesus, "crying with a loud voice, said, 'Father, into your hands I commend my spirit'" (23:46)? Is this something a guilty person would say? Should say? What does convince us that someone charged with a crime and judged guilty by the system is in fact innocent?

While the NRSV translates the centurion's comment as "Certainly this man was innocent," a note indicates that the term could also be translated "righteous." The Greek term underlying the translation is *dikaios*, a word that appears over seventy times in the New Testament. Its primary meaning is "righteous." Had there been an underlying Hebrew, the Hebrew term would be *tzedek*. The term conveys a sense of uprightness of character, fidelity to Torah, generosity to others (the cognate Hebrew term, *tzedakah*, means "charitable giving"). Because righteous people are presumed to be innocent of trespass, the centurion winds up proclaiming Jesus "innocent" in the translations. "Innocent" to me suggests that Jesus was innocent of the charge for which he was condemned; "righteous" holds a host of other connotations, suggesting not just a single charge but a lifetime of good works.

The same term *dikaios* appears elsewhere in Luke's Gospel. For example, it describes Elizabeth and Zechariah (the parents of John the Baptizer [1:6]) and Simeon (the elderly man who witnesses to baby Jesus in the Jerusalem Temple [2:25]). It also, just a few verses down from the centurion's pronouncement, describes Joseph of Arimathea. Here the NRSV gets the better translation, "Now there was a good and *righteous* man named Joseph, who, though a member of the council…" (23:50, emphasis added). His righteous nature will lead to righteous action, as we shall see in chapter 6. In the Book of Acts (Luke's second volume), "righteousness" becomes a key marker of messianic identity. Its first appearance is in Acts 3:13-14, Peter's speech to the population of Jerusalem: "You rejected the Holy and Righteous One…" In Acts 7:52, Stephen explains, "They killed those who foretold the coming of the Righteous One, and now you have become his betrayers and murderers."

The word *righteous* also echoes several passages in the Septuagint, the Greek translation of the Hebrew and Aramaic texts. The term appears close to four hundred times, but one passage in particular provides good intertextual connections.

We've already seen, in our discussions of the other witnesses, connections to Isaiah's co-called "suffering servant" (Isaiah never uses this expression). The most popular Jewish understanding of this servant is the nation of Israel, which suffered in exile in Babylon and then was restored to the homeland. The reading is consistent with passages where Isaiah speaks of "Israel" and "Jacob" as "my servant" (Isaiah 41:8; 44:1, 21; 45:4; 49:3, 5). For the followers of Jesus, *he* was this servant. Isaiah 53:11b describes the servant: "The righteous one, my servant, shall make many righteous, / and he shall bear their iniquities." The label *righteous* reminds readers of Isaiah's suffering servant, regardless of whether the centurion was familiar with Isaiah's prophecy.

There's more to say about calling Jesus *dikaios*. The judgment of Jesus as both righteous and innocent connects the centurion with others who also judge Jesus. Pilate announces three times, "I find no basis for an accusation against this man" (Luke 23:4 cf. 23:14, 22). Herod Antipas can find no charge against him. Dismas states, "This man has done nothing wrong" (Luke 23:41). In the Roman Empire, death by crucifixion was the punishment primarily of enslaved people and rebels. The magnificent 1960 epic *Spartacus* (starring Kirk Douglas and directed by Stanley Kubrick) shows the leader of an uprising against Rome (the "Third Servile War") in 71 BCE—a war that should be better known, especially given attention to the lasting effects of enslavement—dying on a cross. The final scene of Jean Simmons and Peter Ustinov leaving Spartacus then shows crosses lining the road, each with a dying man, each put to death for the sake of freedom.

Luke could not have his readers, like Theophilus to whom the Gospel and Acts are dedicated, thinking of Jesus as either an enslaved man or a rebel. Luke is also being historically accurate, for Jesus was neither a slave nor a military insurrectionist. Thus, Luke has the representative of Rome, the centurion, testify that

Jesus and so his followers were not threats to the empire, or at least not threats by violent revolt.

## Reception History

Developments of the centurion's story do not stop at the cross or in the conversation with Pilate. The soldier who pierces Jesus's side in John enters reception history through an early Christian apocryphal text, called the Acts of Pilate, as Longinus. The name may derive from the Greek word for "lance," the lance or spear that also shows up in legends of the Holy Grail.

In some later versions of his story, he becomes a type of a later Prometheus: living in a cave, he is mauled each night by a lion, he recovers, repeat. More popular is his conflation with the centurion who proclaims Jesus "Son of God" and "righteous/innocent" in the Synoptics. In this tradition, the soldier becomes a Christian and enters the list of saints in the Roman Catholic, Anglican, and various Orthodox communions. In other versions of the story, he was blind, but the blood that flowed from the wound in Jesus's side healed him. In still others, he was martyred in Cappadocia. His statue, by Bernini, is in Saint Peter's Basilica in Rome. He looks good.

The centurion finds his way into more recent work. In George Stephens's 1965 *The Greatest Story Ever Told*, John Wayne (in an uncredited role) plays the centurion at the cross. A legend—since legends beget legends—offers that Stephens directed the Duke to speak with awe, so the Duke recited, "Aww, truly this man was the son of God."

## And Now?

I have my doubts that there was a centurion at the foot of the cross, and there is none in John's Gospel (although as my conservative friends remind me, "Absence of evidence is not evidence of absence"). If he were there, I'm not sure what he said. But the words the Evangelists place on his lips ring true on so many levels.

They speak to Jesus's identity as Son of God, and us at the same time, since we are all children of God. The soldiers remind us that innocent people, for "certainly this man was innocent," are sometimes executed. They remind us that righteous people are sometimes put to death because they acted righteously, actions that others considered threatening.

The centurion challenges us even more. He puts an innocent man to death; he was just following Pilate's orders. And yet he recognizes, although when it is too late to save Jesus, that he was wrong. Jesus in Luke says regarding the soldiers, "Father, forgive them." Can we forgive the centurion and his fellow soldiers too? Can we forgive the individuals in our own time who execute others—in army actions, at traffic stops—and then acknowledge they have done wrong? Or can we, as my friend Maria Mayo suggests, at least pray that God forgive them, even if we can't?

# Chapter 4

# THE BELOVED DISCIPLE

Describing Jesus's crucifixion, John narrates the following: "When Jesus saw his mother and the disciple whom he loved standing beside her, he said to his mother, 'Woman, here is your son.' Then he said to the disciple, 'Here is your mother.' And from that hour the disciple took her into his own home" (John 19:26-27). Only in the Gospel of John does the "Beloved Disciple," the traditional term for the "one whom Jesus loved" (John 13:23), appear, and only in John's Gospel does Jesus, in his dying moment, entrust to this Beloved Disciple the care of his mother.

These two short verses open up multiple questions and multiple possibilities. On the historical front, scholars are still debating the identity of this otherwise anonymous Beloved Disciple. Is he another figure from the Gospel, such as the apostle John, to whom the Gospel is attributed? Is he Lazarus, whom Jesus "loved" (John 11:5) along with his sisters Mary and Martha? Is he Mary Magdalene (a view based not only on novels such as *The Da Vinci Code* but also grounded in recognition both of Mary Magdalene's fidelity and of the greater likelihood of a male versus a female author gaining an audience)? Is he a composite figure representing who any disciple could be or should be? Is his anonymity to be compared to the anonymity of others in the Fourth Gospel, including the mother of Jesus?

On theological and pastoral fronts, the Beloved Disciple signals, among other matters, the beginning of a new family gathered in Jesus's name, the responsibility of the younger generation to care for the elders of the community, and, by extension, the role of that next generation in preserving tradition. Once again, the question of memory surfaces: What stories do we remember of those at the cross, and do we want to remember Jesus as suffering or as in control, as engaging with strangers or speaking to those closest to him? The Gospels offer us choices, and the stories need not be mutually exclusive.

John's Beloved Disciple appears a few other times, and in each case, his role is both enigmatic and filled with potential. Like the woman who anoints Jesus at the home of Simon in Mark 14, the centurion at the cross, and the two thieves crucified on Jesus's left hand and right hand, he shows that important roles are often played by unnamed actors. The lack of name allows us to focus on what the character does or how he is known. For example, the person who founded the community at Qumran, where the Dead Sea Scrolls were discovered, is known in the scrolls only as the "Teacher of Righteousness" (references to "righteousness" should sound familiar after the discussion of Luke's centurion in the last chapter). The Gospels, too, came to us originally from unknown authors. This is not to say that Matthew and John the apostles, John Mark the companion of Peter, and Luke the friend of Paul were not the actual authors, although I have my doubts. But anonymity need not diminish the value of the testimony. Anonymous authorship places emphasis not on the one presenting the material but on the material itself. The anonymous author of the Fourth Gospel we know as a *disciple*, and he was *loved by Jesus*. Can't do much better.

We might wonder: if our names were unknown, by what titles or descriptions would we want to be remembered? As parent or child, teacher or artist, activist or soldier? As beloved or loving, passionate or compassionate? The Beloved Disciple's very anonymity prompts us to question our own self-identification as well as how we identify others, and we're only in the chapter's fifth paragraph.

## The Beloved Disciple in John's Gospel

Although he may have been with Jesus since the calling of the first disciples in John 1, or at the wedding at Cana in chapter 2, we meet the Beloved Disciple explicitly only in John 13, at the Last Supper. Jesus had just predicted, "One of you will betray me" (John 13:21). The disciples are understandably confused. John suddenly notes, "One of his disciples—the one whom Jesus loved—was reclining next to him" (John 13:23).

I have found this comment annoying. The *one he loved*? What are the other disciples, chopped liver? Isn't Jesus supposed to love everyone? John 3:16a reports that "For God so loved the world that he gave his only Son," but Jesus loved just one disciple? Granted, the disciples can be obtuse. Jesus has just noted that one will betray him, and the rest—including the Beloved Disciple—are clueless. But really. The Contemporary English Version translates, "Jesus' favorite disciple was sitting next to him at the meal." Jesus plays favorites? I'm not any happier with this approach.

On the other hand, if we do take Jesus as a human being, then he likely did have favorites. I admit to liking some students more than others—the ones who try harder; the ones who do the work rather attempt to slide through on their charm; the ones who seek new insight rather than parrot back what others have said.

Here's how I've more or less made peace with the idea that Jesus has a BFF (a "best friend forever"). This Beloved Disciple could be any one of us. We all need at one time or another to feel special; we all need now and then to feel an abounding love focused specifically on us. I think John the Evangelist is telling us that we, as individuals, should identify with this fellow. We can all feel as if we are leaning on Jesus, at the Last Supper, and we can all feel as he is speaking directly to us from the cross. (I've asked John whether he intended this interpretation; in my imagination, he smiles back at me.)

I'm still not happy about this verse; it would have been better if John had written something like "One of his disciples—the one whose chicken soup Jesus loved" or "One of his disciples—the one who gave him the idea about the foot-washing." Moving on.

I also find the translation "was reclining next to him" annoying (I should write after I've had a cup of decaf and relaxed a bit more). The Beloved Disciple is reclining on Jesus's breast—a position of intimacy, as we see, for example, in the parable of the rich man and Lazarus, where Lazarus is resting on the bosom of Abraham (Luke 16:23). The NRSV translates, in a bowdlerized manner, that Lazarus is "by his side." The King James Version, closer to the Greek, has "Lazarus in his bosom." Some English translations have the hesitancy to use terms like "breast" or "bosom" and so offer less-intimate terms. Some of these English translations suggest an embarrassment with male friendship and male bodies in proximity.

This scene does give rise to the various legends suggesting the Beloved Disciple was a woman, and to speculation that The *Last Supper*, Da Vinci's painting completed in the 1490s, portrayed the Beloved Disciple in female form, perhaps to indicate Mary Magdalene. Had Da Vinci wanted to paint the figure as Mary Magdalene, he had precedent. Fra Angelico included Mary Magdalene in his 1442 depiction. Had Da Vinci wished to suggest a romantic rather than platonic-intimate relationship between Jesus and any of the disciples, he could have done this as well with any number of symbols. Rather, Da Vinci was being conventional. In art, depictions of Saint John, seen as the author of the Fourth Gospel, are typically of a younger man, often beardless and sometimes even androgynous; they suggest a sensitive, aesthetic bearing. One excellent example is the 1611 *Saint John the Evangelist* by Peter Paul Rubens.

Art is a powerful means of biblical interpretation, and for centuries it taught illiterate people their Bible stories. Many of us, myself included, when we hear the term *Last Supper* cannot help but think of the Da Vinci portrait (I also think of the Mel Brooks version, which both explains why all the men are seated on one side of the table and makes the inquiry, "Separate checks?"). While Da Vinci's setting is terrific if one wants to see the faces of all thirteen men at the supper, it is neither historically credible nor practical in terms of space. Rooms could be rented throughout the Roman Empire for dinner parties; the standard seating was that of a triclinium: three dining couches forming three-fourths of a square or rectangle, with a table in the center. Art can instruct, but it can also mislead.

We had been talking about John 13:21, when Jesus predicted, "One of you will betray me." Following the note about the Disciple's status and position, the Fourth Gospel turns to Peter, ever one to take the initiative even if he does not always follow through. Peter motions to the Beloved Disciple so that he could get the details (John 13:24). The Beloved Disciple, on cue, asks, "Lord, who is it?" (John 13:25). Since it is often helpful to pay attention to a character's first words, then the Disciple's "Lord" is a good place to begin. He prefaces his comments with confession. Then he asks a question; good for him! That is what disciples are supposed to do. That is part of the learning process. More, our Beloved Disciple does not judge (he could have said, something like "Judas is looking a little squirrely, and I was wondering about the money he was supposed to be saving"). Nor does he immediately deny the possibility that he could be the betrayer. We are all capable of wondrous deeds of compassion and heinous deeds of selfishness.

The more I think of it, the more I'm liking this Disciple too. He then fades from the scene as Jesus hands a morsel of bread to Judas and then begins what are called the Last Supper Discourses.

We may pick up the Beloved Disciple next (here's the problem with anonymity) when, according to John 18:15, "Simon Peter and another disciple followed Jesus. Since that disciple was known to the high priest, he went with Jesus into the courtyard of the high priest." We do not know if this "other disciple" is our Beloved Disciple. If so, he's got connections, which may explain why he was not afraid to be at the cross. Scholars are (of course) divided on the identity of this "other disciple": the Beloved Disciple, another previously unmentioned fellow, Nicodemus, even Judas. There's not much more we can do with this anonymous companion of Peter, other than to use our imaginations. I imagine that while Peter is busy denying Jesus in the high priest's courtyard, the Beloved Disciple is making plans with Joseph of Arimathea and Nicodemus to protect Jesus as best they can, but that's my imagination, not John's Gospel.

We definitely meet the Beloved Disciple again in chapter 19, at the cross, and then two more times in the context of Jesus's resurrection appearances. Skipping ahead, we find him for the third (or fourth) time in John 20:2-10. Mary Magdalene had gone to Jesus's tomb, where she sees that the stone had been removed. She runs to Simon Peter and "the other disciple, the one whom Jesus loved" (John 20:2), to report, "They have taken the Lord out of the tomb, and we do not know where they have laid him" (that "we" could be a holdover from the Synoptic accounts, where Mary is accompanied by other women to the tomb; in John's Gospel, she is the only woman explicitly noted as being at the tomb).

Peter and the Beloved Disciple run to the tomb, "but the other disciple outran Peter and reached the tomb first" (John 20:4). For John, the Beloved Disciple always bests Peter: as good as Peter is, the Beloved Disciple is better. Some scholars suggest that Peter represents the Synoptic tradition and especially Matthew, where Peter receives the "keys of the kingdom" (Matthew 16:19), while the Beloved Disciple represents those who look first to the Gospel of John. Today, we may well have our favorite Gospel, but the people who put the canon together insisted that all four must be considered, and each can be used to interpret the others. If we had only John, we would not know about the parables, the exorcisms, or the Sermon on the Mount. If we had only the Synoptics, we would not know that the "Word became flesh," that Jesus wept at Lazarus's tomb, or that Jesus washed the feet of the disciples.

## The Fate of the Beloved Disciple

Peter inquired about the fate of the Disciple Jesus loved. Jesus dismisses the question: "If it is my will that he remain until I come, what is that to you [literally, 'What to you']?" (John 21:22). Jesus dismisses Peter as he had earlier dismissed his mother at Cana by asking, "What concern is that to you and to me?" (John 2:4), when she mentioned that the hosts had run out of wine. The Greek idioms convey the sense of "What concern is that of yours?" or even "So what?" Jesus punctuates this dismissal by commanding Peter, "Follow me!"

This is not the end of the story. It appears that the people responsible for the Gospel we assign to the apostle John, the son of Zebedee, believed that their leader would live until Jesus returned. Thus, John 21:23 reads, "So the rumor spread in the community [literally, 'among the brothers'] that this disciple would not die. Yet Jesus did not say to him that he would not die, but, 'If it is my will that he remain until I come, what is that to you?'" The suggestion that some of Jesus's original followers would not die before their Lord returned in glory appears in other New Testament verses. Matthew 16:28 depicts Jesus as saying, "There are some standing here who will not taste death before they see the Son of Man coming in his kingdom" (also Mark 13:30), and Paul promises, "For this we declare to you by the word of the Lord, that we who are alive, who are left until the coming of the Lord, will by no means precede those who have died" (1 Thessalonians 4:15). Jesus did not return as expected, and his followers, appropriately, recalibrated.

The Beloved Disciple did die. We all do. But the Beloved Disciple leaves his imprint in the words of an anonymous follower, in the Gospel's penultimate line. "This is the disciple who is testifying to these things and has written them, and we [we, John's followers] know that his testimony is true" (John 21:24). The Beloved Disciple, according to this ending, was with Jesus from the beginning of his signs in the Galilee; he was at Cana; he was in the Temple when Jesus healed the paralyzed man; he stayed with Jesus after the feeding of the five thousand, when others deserted him over his statement about eating his flesh and drinking his blood; he watched as the man born blind gained his sight; he witnessed the raising of Lazarus; he rested on Jesus's breast and allowed Jesus to wash his feet. He remained with Jesus at the cross, and after his resurrection.

Christian legend beginning as early as the second-century church father Irenaeus suggests that the Beloved Disciple, identified as John, had a home in Ephesus. After Pentecost, there he brought the mother of Jesus and there he lived a long life of evangelism and died—miraculously, given the traditional fates of all the other apostles—of natural causes.

Now that we have a picture of this faithful witness, this Beloved Disciple, we can better understand how to interpret his role at the cross.

*When Jesus saw his mother and the disciple whom he loved standing beside her, he said to his mother, "Woman, here is your son." Then he said to the disciple, "Here is your mother" (John 19:26–27a).*

In our next chapter, we'll look in greater depth at John's depiction of the mother of Jesus. Here we look at "the disciple whom he loved" to see how this love impacts more than just the Disciple himself, the need for support in times of tragedy, the role of what anthropologists call "fictive kinship," and the import of what are known as "blended families."

John recounts the presence of several individuals "standing near the cross" including Jesus's mother, his mother's sister, Mary the wife of Clopas [who may be his mother's sister], and Mary Magdalene (John 19:25). We do not know about the Beloved Disciple's presence through the narrator's overview. Instead, we see him through Jesus's eyes, as Jesus sees his mother and then the Disciple "standing beside her."

I think that John wants to portray the Disciple's presence as a corrective to the Synoptic tradition. Mark made it clear that at Jesus's arrest in Gethsemane, "All of them [i.e., the disciples] deserted him and fled" (Mark 14:50), and Matthew agrees. Luke begins the process of rehabilitating the male disciples: "But all his acquaintances, including the women who had followed him from Galilee, stood at a distance, watching these things" (Luke 23:49). These "acquaintances" include the men who fled from the arrest. John's Gospel, conversely, insists that they did not all forsake him and flee. They did not all stay at a distance. The Beloved Disciple stayed the course and remained at the cross, close enough for Jesus to see him and to talk with him. Jesus is most definitely not alone as he dies.

This break between what the narrator of the Fourth Gospel sees and what Jesus sees suggests to me not just a correction to the Synoptics but also that God sees more than any human would and that God recognizes those whom others would overlook. (I asked John about this reading; he told me he liked it.) There's a comfort to being seen through Jesus's eyes, and there's a blessing to know that we are seen doing what we should be doing in terms of caring for those who love us.

I appreciate John, as he frequently corrects moments in the Synoptics that disturb me. For example, after that difficult moment in Luke 10:38-42, where Martha complains about how much serving (the Greek term gives us the English word "deacon") she has to do and Jesus informs her that her sister Mary has chosen the better part, Mary and Martha never speak with each other. The tension between the sisters is never resolved. In John 11–12, the sisters work as a team. Or for another example, according to Matthew 10:5b, the disciples are not to evangelize the Samaritans. In John 4, Jesus rectifies that gap by speaking with the Samaritan woman and then meeting with the people in her town while the disciples are getting lunch. A third: Mark suggests that the entire Sanhedrin voted to condemn Jesus, but John has Joseph of Arimathea and Nicodemus representing those who supported him.

By showing how Jesus takes special notice of the Beloved Disciple, John also reminds us of all the other anonymous witnesses who have gone unnoticed from antiquity to today by the people who are writing history. If we look through his eyes, we focus differently. At all the people who are around us, on whom do our eyes fall? Who needs to be noticed, and acknowledged, at this particular moment? When I go to visit my mother-in-law in the assisted living facility, and I am looking for her, I make a point of noticing, and thanking as well, the compassionate professionals who provide her the medical care and the daily companionship that I cannot.

The Beloved Disciple and the mother gain strength from each other, and they also gain strength from Jesus, who is controlling the events around him. John's Jesus does not cry out, "My God, my God, why have you forsaken me"; the Fourth Gospel depicts no conversation between Jesus and the two other victims executed with him. In John's account, Jesus attends to his own, and he does so from his position as uplifted Lord. He commands both his mother and the Disciple, "See!" "Look!" His eyes on each of them, he commands them to turn away from looking at him and to look at each other. We can see (to continue the visual focus) Jesus as here setting up a new family, not based in biology and not based in marriage or adoption but based on another new commandment. He is forcing our eyes, and our focus, from the past to a new future, where relationship is fully grounded in a love not determined by biology or marital status, but by relationship to him.

By mentioning at the cross that this is the Disciple whom Jesus "loved," the Fourth Gospel also sends us back to the farewell discourses in chapter 13, where Jesus issues another commandment, a "new commandment." John 13:34 reads, "I give you a new commandment, that you love each other. Just as I have loved you, you also should love one another." There is nothing new about the command to love one another; that was already established in Leviticus, with the commandments regarding love of neighbor (Leviticus 19:18) and love of stranger (Leviticus 19:34). Nor is John talking about love of enemies. The focus in this discourse is on how the love displayed by his disciples for each other works: "By this everyone will know that you are my disciples, if you have love for one another" (John 13:35). John is not talking about emotive love; *love* here means a practical stance, an action. Taking an older woman into one's house and guaranteeing her support for the rest of her life is this new commandment in action. The mother's obedience to this commandment, which we see in the next chapter, also shows the commandment in action. The Beloved Disciple and the mother will love each other, and they will continue to comfort each other. Part of that comfort is the memory of how Jesus loved them and cared for them.

The Beloved Disciple will do what he can to console the mother of Jesus by becoming a new son to her. One child can never replace the child who has died. But that second child can comfort and support. Memories of the dead are not replaced, but they can be supplemented. When the second child reminds the mother (any parent) of the first, by action or saying or even mannerism, there can be a sense of peace. When Jesus told his disciples to love one another as he had loved them, he did so knowing that he would not be with them forever. Immediately prior to the love command, he informed them, "Where I am going, you cannot come" (John 13:33). The Beloved Disciple, in obedience to Jesus's command, will welcome Jesus's mother not as a stranger, and not even as the mother of Jesus, but as his own mother. He cannot go where Jesus has gone, but he can live as Jesus would have wanted him to live. So can we all.

## And Now?

### *From that hour the disciple took her into his own home (John 19:27b).*

From that hour! A few early manuscripts read "day" rather than "hour," but "hour" is one of John's favorite terms. Technically, "hour" is a temporal marker. The narrative time is about noon or, from the Greek, "about the sixth hour" (John 19:14). But in terms of literature, the timing is one of moving from one era to another. Throughout the Gospel, Jesus has been speaking about his "hour," and the first time, he mentioned it to his mother. When she approaches him about the lack of wine at the wedding, he tells her that his "hour" had not yet come (John 2:4). The sign of the healing of the royal official's son is punctuated by references to the "hour" (John 4:52, 53); Jesus predicts that the "hour is coming, and is now here, when the dead will hear the voice of the Son of God and those who hear will live" (John 5:25; cf. 5:28). His arrest cannot occur while he is still teaching "because his hour had not yet come" (John 7:30; 8:20), and finally as the Passion begins, so does his hour, his glorification (John 12:23, 27; 13:1; 17:1, and others).

The last reference to the hour is here at the cross, when the Beloved Disciple takes the mother of Jesus into his home. There is glorification not only in Jesus's being lifted up; there is glorification in the Beloved Disciple's acting on this last command Jesus will give before he dies. Just as wind can be the Spirit, as running water can be living water, as one can be both born and born anew, so even time can be sacralized. Any hour can be the time when discipleship is recognized in love. The next time someone asks you, "What time is it?" and you see the hour, these verses from John might echo in your mind. If they do, you've moved from clock time to sacred time.

John 19:27b can suggest that the Beloved Disciple and the mother of Jesus, in that hour, left the body of Jesus on the cross. The reading can explain why these two people, closest to Jesus, did not take his body from the cross themselves. I'd prefer to think that they remained to the end, and then helped in the disposition. That is how Christian tradition remembers the story, as best exemplified in Michelangelo's statue, the *Pietà*.

The Greek of John 19:27b states that the Disciple took the mother to his "own"—the translation "home" shows an understanding of the Greek idiom (the same expression appears in John 1:11; 16:32). "His own" is the place where one finds oneself at home, safe, comfortable, unalienated. Earlier, Jesus told his followers, "The hour is coming, indeed it has come, when you will be scattered, each one to his home, and you will leave me alone. Yet I am not alone because the Father is with me" (John 16:32). While "being scattered" does sound negative—the same term appears in the Good Shepherd discourse of chapter 10, where Jesus describes the wolf who snatches and "scatters" the sheep— here it, too, can take on new meaning: separate families, but families who unite in concern and in faith. For this new community, in John's view, their "own"—the place they can call their country or their home—will be where people will gather in the name of Jesus for "the hour is coming, and is now here, when the true worshipers will worship the Father in spirit and truth" (John 4:23).

# Chapter 5

# THE WOMEN

Women had been both supporters of Jesus and beneficiaries of his healings and exorcisms since the beginning of his public mission. In Galilee, Peter's mother-in-law, whom Jesus had healed of a fever, "ministered" to him (the Greek term, *diakonein*, is the source of the English term "deacon"; see Matthew 8:14-15; Mark 1:30-31). Jesus restores a hemorrhaging woman to both health and ritual purity by stopping her bleeding; he resuscitates a twelve-year-old girl; he raises up a woman bent over from osteoporosis (Luke says she is bent over by Satan, which is not mutually exclusive to osteoporosis); he exorcises seven demons from Mary Magdalene and from the daughter of a Gentile woman. Like Peter's mother-in-law, Martha engages in ministry (*diakonein* again) while her sister Mary listens to Jesus's teaching (so Luke 10:38-42), and in John's Gospel, Martha confesses Jesus to be the Messiah while Mary anoints his feet (John 11–12). Jesus engages with a Samaritan woman at a well and with the daughters of Jerusalem on the way to the cross. According to Luke 8:2b-3, "Some women who had been cured of evil spirits and infirmities: Mary, called Magdalene, from whom seven demons had gone out, and Joanna, the wife of Herod's steward Chuza, and Susanna, and many others provided for them [other manuscripts read "him," that is, Jesus] out of their resources." Elizabeth is with Mary prior to Jesus's birth; the prophet Anna greets him in the Temple, and women are with him at the cross and at the tomb.

Despite these and other stories of Jesus's interactions with women, the Gospels threaten to give a sense that women's presence in Jesus's company is inconsistent. The women can seem like guest stars at a concert or on a television show: if we miss the performance or the episode, we would not know they had been there. While we can follow Jesus and his male disciples from chapter to chapter, Peter's mother-in-law gets only two verses; in Luke's Gospel, Mary and Martha get four.

The corrective to this impression of women's spotty appearances is in how we read the Gospels. In the synagogue, when we get to the end of Deuteronomy, we rewind the Torah scroll and begin again with Genesis. Each time we reread, we draw upon what we remember from our past encounters with the text. So too, when we get to the end of each Gospel, we should return to the beginning, and then we see with what might be called "resurrection eyes": we see hints of what will be; we find new meaning in what had already been recounted. The Gospel of John even suggests such retrospective reading: "His disciples did not understand these things at first; but when Jesus was glorified, *then they remembered* that these things had been written of him and had been done to him" (12:16, emphasis added). When we read the Gospels through and then return for a second (and third, and fourth) visit, we correct or supplement or even replace earlier impressions.

To the first impression that women are only sporadically part of the story, Mark provides a corrective: at the cross—*at the cross! at the end of chapter 15 of a 16-chapter Gospel!*—Mark laconically mentions, following the centurion's confession "Truly this man was God's son," that "there were also women looking on from a distance; among them were Mary Magdalene, and Mary the mother of James the younger and of Joses, and Salome. These used to follow him and provided for him when he was in Galilee, and there were many other women who had come up with him to Jerusalem" (15:40-41). The women had been with Jesus the entire time, from his days in Galilee to his final week in Jerusalem. Thanks, Mark; better late than never. Now when we read Mark again, we see the women at the healings, the teachings, and the controversies. They were there the entire time.

The Gospel writers all agree that there were women at the cross, but the details they record are not always consistent. Similarly, the Evangelists recorded that women were part of Jesus's ministry, serving and being served, but they provide different details. Regarding the witnesses at the cross, Mary Magdalene's presence at the cross as well as the empty tomb is consistent across the four canonical Gospels. The names of the other women change, and their identifications have been debated across the centuries.

Trying to figure out who the various women witnesses to the cross are gives me a headache. However, since such figuring is what biblical scholars do, and since I know some people are fascinated by the process of disentangling these women, here are the details (feel free to skip the next several paragraphs, or make a scorecard). Mark 15:40 mentions "Mary Magdalene, and Mary the mother of James the younger and of Joses, and Salome." It is possible that "Mary the mother of James and Joses" is a reference to Mary the mother of Jesus, since according to Mark 6:3, Jesus has four brothers, "*James* and *Joses* and Judas and Simon" (emphasis added).

If this first Mary is Jesus's mother, then Mark has, subtly, indicated that Mary has joined the movement despite earlier accounts that she had not. By identifying Mary in terms of her other children (biological children or children of Joseph's by a previous marriage, or nephews—the relationship depends on what one believes concerning the extent of Mary's virginity; sorting that question generally depends on the church one attends; Mark's Gospel lacks the narrative of the virginal conception, so Mary's sexual status is not a concern in this text), Mark signals that she is important not because she is the mother of Jesus but because she is a disciple. The theology here is fine, but the explanation strikes me as convoluted.

Only John explicitly places the mother of Jesus at the cross, and the Evangelist Luke, in the Book of Acts (1:14), indicates that Mary was with the followers in Jerusalem in the days after Jesus's death. Later tradition, especially among the church fathers who write in Syriac, insists that Mary the mother of Jesus was not only present at the cross; she was also present at the tomb. The accounts preserved in the Gospels gave rise to new speculation, and so the stories continue to develop across the centuries.

We do not know who Salome of Mark 15:40 is, but Matthew may provide a hint. Matthew, likely using Mark as a source, agrees that there were many women at the cross, watching from a distance, and that they had provided for Jesus. But the names change: Matthew lists Mary Magdalene, but then instead of Mark's "Mary the mother of James the younger and of Joses," Matthew gives us "Mary the mother of James and Joseph." Matthew 13:55 names Jesus's brothers "*James* and *Joseph* and Simon and Judas" (emphasis added) so perhaps Matthew thought this Mary was Jesus's mother. This still seems a convoluted way of locating Mary the mother of Jesus at the cross.

Then, Matthew lists "the mother of the sons of Zebedee" (Matthew 27:56). The "sons of Zebedee" are the apostles James and John, part of the inner circle along with Peter. Gone is Mark's Salome, unless "Salome" is the first name of Mrs. Zebedee. It may well have been. Along with the name Mary (Miriam, Mariamme, Maryam, and other variants), Salome (from the Hebrew, *shalom*) was an exceptionally popular name for first-century Jewish women in Galilee and Judea. Although the Gospels never name the daughter of Herodias, who danced for Herod Antipas and received as a prize the head of John the Baptizer on a silver platter, a hint from Josephus names her Salome, and the name became secured with Oscar Wilde's one-act play *Salome* (1891; you may have seen Aubrey Beardsley's illustrations) and then Richard Strauss's 1905 opera *Salome* based on Wilde's play. The name likely gained popularity among first-century Jewish families from the Jewish Queen Salome Alexandra (also known as Shalomtzion, meaning "peace of Zion") who ruled 76-67 BCE. Was Mrs. Zebedee named Salome? The odds are in favor of Mary or Salome (just as in 1980, Jennifer and Jessica were top of the list).

In Luke's account, there are women not only at the cross but on what has become known as the Via Dolorosa, the "Sorrowful Way" or "Way of Suffering," the route the soldiers force Jesus to walk from Pilate's trial to Golgotha. Luke reports that "a great number of the people followed him, and among them were women who were beating their breasts and wailing for him" (Luke 23:27). Following Jesus's conversation with the "good thief" and the centurion's proclamation of Jesus's righteousness/innocence, Luke announces, "When all the crowds who had gathered there for this spectacle saw what had taken place, they returned home, beating their breasts. But all his acquaintances, including the women who had followed him from Galilee, stood at a distance, watching these things" (Luke 23:48-49). Thus Luke offers two groups of women. As for the now-familiar Galilean contingent, Luke does not name them until their report to the disciples concerning the empty tomb and the proclamation of Jesus's resurrection. These women, according to Luke, were "Mary Magdalene, Joanna, Mary the mother of James, and the other women with them who told this to the apostles" (Luke 24:10). Is Mary the mother of James the same woman as Mark's "Mary the mother of James the younger and of Joses," and Matthew's "Mary the mother of James and Joseph"? My head is now pounding and I'm in search of a hot compress.

Finally, John's Gospel reports, "Standing near the cross of Jesus were his mother, and his mother's sister, Mary the wife of Clopas, and Mary Magdalene" (19:25b). Perhaps John stations four women—the mother, the mother's sister (unnamed), Mary the wife of Clopas, and Mary Magdalene—or three women, with Mary the wife of Clopas being the sister of Jesus's mother. Maybe she's named Salome? There are times I think I should have gone to law school, as my mother advised.

According to John, Jesus sees his mother (as we've seen, she's never named in the Fourth Gospel) and the Disciple "whom he loved"; he tells his mother, "Woman, here is your son," and the Beloved Disciple, "Here is your mother" (John 19:25b-27). John, who adapted material in the Synoptic Gospels to bring a sense of completion to several narratives, does so again here by making explicit points only hinted at in the Synoptics: that the mother of Jesus was a faithful follower, and that Jesus specifically recognized her fidelity.

The women at the cross have different stories to tell in each Gospel. As we hear the stories of Mary the mother of Jesus, Mary Magdalene, the mother of the sons of Zebedee, the daughters of Jerusalem, and others, we can see the relationship of discipleship to the new family gathered in Jesus's name, the patronage role women served in the movement, and the continuity between the cross and the tomb. The women at the cross prompt us to reflect on the other women in the Gospels, and they point us forward to parents who lose their children to violence, to disciples determined to carry on the good news, to insiders and outsiders, and more.

## Named and Unnamed Women in Mark's Version

Mark describes women "looking on from a distance" but only names three: "Mary Magdalene, and Mary the mother of James the younger and of Joses, and Salome" (Mark 15:40). Perhaps the named women were known to people to whom Mark would give the Gospel text, just as that audience may have known Alexander and Rufus, the children of Simon of Cyrene, whom Mark also mentions (Mark 15:21). But more is going on here than ancient name-dropping.

Some commentators see an echo here of Psalm 38:11, "My friends and companions stand aloof from my affliction, / and my neighbors stand far off." I do not sense that the women are "aloof from" Jesus's affliction. There are other, better, reasons to stand at a distance. Perhaps the women are afraid, lest the soldiers who execute Jesus would execute them as well. Perhaps they are not ignoring his pain but shielding themselves from it. Some things are just too hard to see. Some of us do not want to make the hospital or hospice visit; we prefer to remember our loved ones as they were, in better days. Perhaps the women feel unworthy to come closer: Should they have fought harder to keep him from being condemned? Should they have shown more support? What had they failed to do, only to think that whatever it was, it is now too late? The women's placement, and the lack of explanation for it, serves to interrogate our own behaviors at such moments.

On a practical level, Mary Magdalene and the other women provide continuity from the Deposition to the body's placement in the tomb. Mark 15:46-47 explains that Joseph of Arimathea took the body from the cross, wrapped it in the linen cloth, placed it in a rock-cut tomb and sealed the tomb with a stone against the door of the tomb, and that "Mary Magdalene and Mary the mother of

Joses were observing where he was laid." Thus, the women had to have been close enough to follow Joseph from Golgotha to the tomb. Then they do more than witness.

In Mark's Gospel, these same three named women seek to attend to Jesus's body: "When the Sabbath was over," they "bought spices, so that they might go and anoint him" (16:1). The problem: in Mark's Gospel, Jesus had already been anointed. Mark recounts how, while Jesus is reclining at table at the home of Simon, in Bethany, "a woman came with an alabaster jar of very costly ointment of nard, and she broke open the jar and poured the ointment on his head" (Mark 14:3). When some of the people at the dinner complained at this extravagance, since the cost of the perfume could have supported a family for half a year, Jesus rebukes them, "Let her alone; why do you trouble her? . . . For you always have the poor with you, and you can show kindness to them whenever you wish; but you will not always have me. She has done what she could; she has anointed my body beforehand for its burial" (Mark 14:6-8). Jesus has already been anointed. The named women who come to the tomb are too late.

Not only are Mark's women attempting a redundant act, but also they appear inept. As they head to the tomb, they begin to ask, "Who will roll away the stone for us from the entrance to the tomb?" (Mark 16:3)—bad planning on their part. Next, the "young man" (he's really an angel) they encounter at the tomb berates them, "But go, tell his disciples and Peter that he is going ahead of you to Galilee; there you will see him, *just as he told you*" (Mark 16:7, emphasis added). Jesus had announced, as he was leaving the Last Supper and heading toward the Mount of Olives, "But after I am raised up, I will go before you to Galilee" (Mark 14:28). Thanks Mark: we now must write the women back into that story as well. If they had heard this prediction, like the male disciples, they did not believe it.

Most scholars (including me) agree that Mark's Gospel originally ended at 16:8; the final verse of the Gospel. That last verse confirms the women's failure: "So they went out and fled from the tomb, for terror and amazement had seized them; and they said nothing to anyone, for they were afraid." Mark, and Mark's readers, know that the proclamation of Jesus's resurrection was made. It is for the readers to do what the women, at least initially, failed to do.

The three named women, who had been with Jesus since his days in Galilee, are too late with the spices, unprepared on their way to the tomb, and unwilling or unable to proclaim the good news. But—and here is a marvelous indicator of Mark's genius—Mark has provided these three named women three male counterparts, equally named and equally having failed, until we move past the Gospel narrative and into the future. In Gethsemane, three named disciples—Peter, James, and John—fail Jesus; they fail to remain awake with him; they fail to keep watch for him; they fail to support him after he is arrested. Two simply disappear and one exacerbates his failures in Gethsemane by denying Jesus three times in the high priest's court. But we know that their failures are not the end of the story. Jesus cries out in Mark the first verse of Psalm 22, "My God, my God, why have you forsaken me?" But that is not the end of this psalm. We continue the story onward from Mark 16:8 to know that God had not forsaken Jesus, just as we readers fill in the last lines of Psalm 22: "Posterity will serve him; / future generations will be told about the Lord, / and proclaim his deliverance to a people yet unborn, / saying that he has done it" (Psalm 22:30-31). It is up to us readers to fill in the rest of the stories of Peter, James, and John, Mary Magdalene, the other Mary, and Salome.

There is more (Mark is such a good writer!). In contrast to the named figures, two anonymous figures, a man and a woman, reveal themselves fully aware. An anonymous woman, despite rejection by Jesus's other table companions, anoints Jesus for his burial. An anonymous centurion at the cross, despite his employ by the Roman Empire whose leaders were considered divine, proclaims Jesus "God's Son" (Mark 15:39).

Attend, Mark tells us: the named figures are disciples, and they were doing their best although they failed. You, too, may be a prominent member in the community, and you may fail, but the Gospel will still be proclaimed, and you can have a part in it, just as do Peter, James, and John, Mary Magdalene, Mary the mother of James, and Salome. Next, attend to the nameless saints among you: the strangers who perceive more than the insiders because they can see with fresh eyes; people from other cultures who interpret events in new and profound ways. Be open to the others in the community, remember their names, listen to their stories, and learn from them.

## Mrs. Zebedee and the Other Women in Matthew's Version

Describing the women at the cross and tomb, Matthew changes the details. In this second account (again, Matthew is likely using Mark as a source), the women at the cross include "Mary Magdalene, and Mary the mother of James and Joseph, and the mother of the sons of Zebedee" (Matthew 27:56). The second Mary could be Jesus's mother, or not. The "mother of the sons of Zebedee" could be the "Salome" mentioned in Mark's account. Or not. We can do more interesting, and less frustrating, work.

We can start with Mrs. Zebedee (did I mention that I like her?). We met her husband at the beginning of Jesus's public ministry. Matthew 4:21-22 records that Jesus, after encountering Peter and Andrew and so gaining his first two disciples, "saw two other brothers, James son of Zebedee and his brother John, in the boat with their father Zebedee, mending their nets, and he called them. Immediately they left the boat and their father, and followed him." Were I Zebedee, seeing this stranger calling my kids away from the family business, I would not be pleased. We can imagine Zebedee trying to explain to his wife what had happened, and then Mrs. Zebedee rushing off to bring her boys home. But hearing the boys talk about Jesus, and then hearing Jesus herself, Mrs. Zebedee decides that she will stay to hear more and see more (and to keep an eye on James and John, known for being somewhat hotheaded).

The New Testament gives us no indication that Zebedee, the dad, joined the movement. The Gospels suggest that Jesus held a greater appeal for the middle generation, for adult sons rather than fathers or their children. For example, Matthew 8:21 (and see Luke 9:59) recounts how a disciple asked Jesus, "Lord, first let me go and bury my father" (the reference is likely to secondary burial, the practice of collecting the bones of the deceased, a year after the death, and placing the bones in an ossuary, literally a "bone" box). Jesus declines the request.

Jesus's appeal to women lacks this generational focus, but the tradition does pay attention to marital status. Mrs. Zebedee would not be the only wife who, apart from her husband, found herself among Jesus's followers. According to Luke 8:3, Joanna the wife of Herod Antipas's estate manager, Chuza, followed Jesus, but Chuza's discipleship goes unmentioned. These married women prompt the question: What happens when the one spouse is a follower of Jesus, and one has competing theological beliefs, or no theological beliefs at all? One wants to go to church, and the other has booked a 9 a.m. tee-off or has a tennis court reserved for 10 o'clock?

Paul offers the best short answer to this difficult situation. In 1 Corinthians, he addresses several practical problems that his

Gentile congregants had posed. One concerns how marriage is to function when one partner has joined the assembly and one has not. Paul writes, "If any woman has a husband who is an unbeliever, and he consents to live with her, she should not divorce him. For the unbelieving husband is made holy through his wife, and the unbelieving wife is made holy through her husband....But if the unbelieving partner separates, let it be so; in such a case the brother or sister is not bound. It is to peace that God has called you" (1 Corinthians 7:13-15).

Mrs. Zebedee's presence at the cross is her second appearance in Matthew's Gospel, and both instances show Matthew expanding Mark's account. According to Mark 10:37, the two sons of Zebedee, John and James, ask Jesus, "Grant us to sit, one at your right hand and one at your left, in your glory." We've seen the irony of this request, since the two on Jesus's right and left hands will be the two men crucified next to him. Matthew changes the story. In Matthew's version, "*the mother* of the sons of Zebedee came to him with her sons, and kneeling before him, she asked a favor of him" (Matthew 20:20, emphasis added; see discussion in chapter 2).

Matthew 27:56 locates Mrs. Zebedee, together with Mary Magdalene and Mary the mother of James and Joseph, at the cross. But Matthew 27:61 notes that only "Mary Magdalene and the other Mary" watched the entombment. Similarly, in reporting on the empty tomb, Matthew 28:1 states, "After the sabbath, as the first day of the week was dawning, Mary Magdalene and the other Mary went to see the tomb." Mrs. Zebedee has gone missing.

At this point, all we can do is use our imagination to explain her absence. Here's my take: I think that Mrs. Zebedee, knowing that her sons had fled Gethsemane and seeing that they were not at the cross, felt it more important to look after the boys rather than anoint Jesus's body. Perhaps she was among the other attendees at Simon's house and heard Jesus speak of how the anonymous woman had anointed him for burial. Perhaps she heard Jesus speak of how, after he was raised, he would greet his disciples in the Galilee. I picture her going back to the Galilee with her sons and the other disciples, and there rallying them. She knew that the cross was not the end of the story. As Mary Magdalene becomes the apostle to the apostles in John's Gospel, so Mrs. Zebedee, the good mom, becomes the apostle to the eleven remaining disciples in my reading of her story in Matthew's Gospel. Perhaps she even convinced Zebedee to listen to a story or two.

While Mrs. Zebedee is (at least in my imagination) journeying north to the Galilee, the other two Marys are at the tomb. Again, Matthew changes the story, and again, Matthew gives these early followers an upgrade. Instead of Mark's three, named, frightened women—in parallel to the three named frightened disciples—Matthew disrupts the connection of the women and the men by naming only two women.

Instead of having the women go to the tomb to anoint the body and worry about who would remove the stone, Matthew changes the plot. In Matthew's version, the women at the cross and the tomb are not inept or redundant, since they do not seek to anoint the body. Rather, Matthew tells us, "After the sabbath, as the first day of the week was dawning, Mary Magdalene and the other Mary went to see the tomb" (Matthew 28:1). The change of motive has at least two practical implications. First, only Matthew reports that the tomb was guarded, so anointing the body would have created problems with the guards. Second, watching tombs is in fact what people did. Grave robbery was a possibility, but also, in the cultural imagination of antiquity, some people thought that the nails and other material aspects of crucifixion held magical power. Watching the tomb would have protected the body from any who would seek to desecrate the corpse, or profit from it.

The women raise for us the question of why we go to a cemetery or visit a grave: to watch, to commemorate, to celebrate a life, or to mourn a death. Did they remember the prediction and expect a miracle? Did they think that they were protecting the dead body, only to learn that the raised body will be for them the source of new life? Did they just go to look, to be present, to remember?

## The Daughters of Jerusalem and the Other Women in Luke's Version

According to Luke 23:27-28, "A great number of the people followed [Jesus], and among them were women who were beating their breasts and wailing for him. But Jesus turned to them and said, 'Daughters of Jerusalem, do not weep for me, but weep for yourselves and for your children.'" These women, along with others, will accompany Jesus to "the place that is called The Skull" (Luke 23:33). The daughters of Jerusalem remind us of such matters as communal responsibility and regret, of the victims of war, and of mothers who will watch their children die because of the greed, selfishness, and privilege of others.

We first find the expression "Daughters of Jerusalem" in the Song of Songs, also known as the Song of Solomon or Canticles. In Song 1:5, the female lover exults, "I am black and beautiful, / O daughters of Jerusalem." In 5:8, she beseeches the "daughters of Jerusalem, / 'If you find my beloved, / tell him this; / I am faint with love'"; and in 5:16 she tells the "daughters of Jerusalem" that "his speech is most sweet, / and he is altogether desirable. / This is my beloved and this is my friend." She will use the same address to this audience, the women of the city, in Song 2:7; 3:5, 10; and 8:4. The only other place this expression appears is in Luke 23:28, where Jesus, not the female lover, adjures the daughters not about love but about loss. I cannot read Luke's verse without thinking of the Song of Solomon. Thus, I associate the daughters of Jerusalem as having a love for Jesus. The language may be erotic, but in antiquity, erotic language could be used to express deep theological yearnings.

Luke 23:27b locates among the crowd on the Via Dolorosa, "women who were beating their breasts and wailing for him." The Greek does not have words for "chest" or "breast" here (how ironic: the translators have no problem inserting the word "breast" here, but they gloss over the word when it refers to the breast of Jesus at the Last Supper). The addition is appropriate since the location of the blows is made explicit in the return home of these followers (Luke 23:48).

To beat one's breast is a sign not only of mourning or lamentation but also of repentance. We can only speculate as to what exactly the women intended with their gesture. Some commentators take the cynical view that beating the breast is what women do, customarily, at a public execution; thus, they are going through the motions of mourning. It seems to me that these women are more than conventional mourners; they are sympathetic to Jesus. Were they just going through motions, there is little reason for Jesus to speak with them. Others suggest that the women represent the Jews of Jerusalem whom Jesus rejects: go mourn for yourself, he tells them. This, too, strikes me as incorrect as well as uncharitable, for Jesus loves the city. He has already told Jerusalem's residents that destruction is coming, and following that destruction, redemption. In Luke 13:35 he states, "See, your house is left to you. And I tell you, you will not see me until the time comes when you say, 'Blessed is the one who comes in the name of the Lord.'" This prediction is not a sign of rejection; it is an indication that the promises to Israel are irrevocable (see Romans 11:29). According to Luke's narrative, when Jesus returns (in triumph) to Jerusalem, there will be Jews there to acknowledge his messianic reign.

There are better understandings of these women. For example, the daughters of Jerusalem could be lamenting the execution of a man they regarded as a prophet and a healer; like Luke's centurion at the cross, they know that Jesus was a "righteous man" or an "innocent man" who was falsely condemned. They could have been lamenting the miscarriage of justice and, behind it, the power of Rome. Their description may allude to Zechariah 12:10, a verse we have already noted in relation to the soldier in John who pierces Jesus's side with a sword: "I will pour out a spirit of compassion and supplication on the house of David and the inhabitants of Jerusalem, so that, when they look on the one whom they have pierced, they shall mourn for him, as one mourns for an only child, and weep bitterly over him, as one weeps over a firstborn." The Hebrew underlying the Greek translation of Zechariah does not read "the one" but "me."

The daughters of Jerusalem could also be repenting. In the Jewish tradition, worshippers on Yom Kippur, the Day of Atonement, recite as a community a litany of sins, and for each sin the tradition is to curl one's hand into a fist and then tap the chest above the heart. "Beating" is not the correct term; the gesture is a tap to remind, not a blow to punish. Since Jewish life is communal, the people who support Jesus also recognize their complicity in what is about to happen. My point is not to blame "the Jews" for the Crucifixion; it is to suggest that communities recognize that actions taken by leaders impact the people as a whole. When a politician voted into office, or a minister hired by a congregation, does something sinful or harmful, the community is impacted, the community may mourn, and the community may also feel a sense of responsibility.

Jesus tells these women that their lamentation is misplaced: "Do not weep for me, but weep for yourselves and for your children" (Luke 23:28). He continues, "Blessed are the childless" for "the days are surely coming when they will say, 'Blessed are the barren, and the wombs that never bore, and the breasts that never nursed'" (Luke 23:29).

In the Sermon on the Mount (so Matthew's Gospel) and the Sermon on the Plain (Luke's version of similar material), Jesus offers what are called *beatitudes* or *makarisms*, such as the familiar "Blessed are the poor in spirit" and "Blessed are the meek." The form is familiar. The *makarism* Jesus pronounces on his way to the cross takes the familiar form but gives it ironic content. At the same time, he alludes to a familiar passage from Isaiah, and reverses that. Isaiah had predicted the recovery of Jerusalem, the "barren woman," following Babylon's razing of the Temple:

> *Sing, O barren one who did not bear;*
>> *burst into song and shout,*
>> *you who have not been in labor!*
> *For the children of the desolate woman will be more*
>> *than the children of her that is married, says the* LORD.
>
> (Isaiah 54:1)

Isaiah blessed the infertile Jerusalem, who will once again teem with life. Jesus now blesses the infertile, for having children will seem more a curse than a blessing.

Isaiah spoke of the aftermath of the Babylonian Exile, when the invaders destroyed the first Temple; Jesus speaks of the forthcoming First Jewish Revolt against Rome, which took place in 66-70 CE, when Roman troops burned down the second Temple. And they did more. The Romans surrounded Jerusalem and cut off the food supplies to starve the people into submission. Josephus reports episodes of women eating their children in order to survive (*Jewish War* 6.205-207; cf. Deuteronomy 28:53). Better to be childless, Jesus suggests, than to watch your children either die of starvation or, if they survive the final Roman siege, be sold into slavery.

The women will not weep alone. While the answer to the trivia question "What is the shortest verse in the Bible?" is John 11:35, "Jesus wept" (KJV; the NRSV lengthens the translation to "Jesus began to weep"), which he does at the tomb of Lazarus, this is not the only Gospel account of Jesus weeping. At the end of his long journey to Jerusalem, which began in Luke 9, the Evangelist remarks that Jesus "came near and saw the city," and "he wept over it, saying, 'If you, even you, had only recognized on this day the things that make for peace! But now they are hidden from your eyes. Indeed, the days will come upon you, when your enemies will set up ramparts around you and surround you and hem you in on every side. They will crush you to the ground, you and your children within you, and they will not leave within you one stone upon another; because you did not recognize the time of your visitation from God'" (Luke 19:41-44).

In Luke's view, the destruction of Jerusalem is a direct result of the people's failure to recognize Jesus as their lord. The claim is a theological one. We search for reasons for disasters, whether personal or local or national. We want people to blame. Sometimes, we feel the need to blame ourselves. Simplistic explanation for wars, forced migrations, genocides, atomic bombs, and the like do a disservice to history. We might therefore speculate on what we can tolerate, and what we find so intolerable that we rise up in rebellion. Do we allow our God to be mocked (that question of blasphemy)? Do we allow Caesar to put his image in the Temple? Do we remain silent when our worship practices are forbidden? We might also ask whether our beliefs and practices are sources for brokering peace or for justifying war. Once again, the Bible helps us ask the right questions.

Before we leave the daughters of Jerusalem, one final notice. Along with a reminder of the destruction of war, Jesus's message to these women has an added note of pathos since according to John's Gospel and the Synoptics as well (depending on how we identify the various Marys at the cross) Jesus's mother will watch her son die. Blessed are the childless, who do not have to watch their children put to death by the state.

After reporting that the crowds who had gathered at the cross, witnessing Jesus's death, "returned home, beating their breasts," Luke returns to the narratives familiar from Mark and Matthew: "But all his acquaintances, including the women who had followed him from Galilee, stood at a distance, watching these things" (Luke 23:49). No names, and now the male disciples can be seen as standing together with the women. In Luke's report of the women witnessing the entombment, again, the names go missing (23:55). The third reference, to the women's visit to the tomb early Sunday morning—as in Mark's account, they are bringing spices—again, no names (Luke 24:1). I get the impression that Luke is toning down the import of the women's witness to the tomb; I have issues with Luke, who has lots of stories about women, but with the exception of the first two chapters, does not give women much agency.

Next, we read that "two men in dazzling clothes" (costume design for angels) meet the women at the tomb and remind them of Jesus's prediction that the Son of Man would "on the third day rise again" (24:4, 7). Adding to Mark's story, Luke remarks that the women "remembered his words" (24:8). The women, reminded of the prediction and convinced by the empty tomb and the angelic commentary that the prediction had come true, return to report what they had seen and heard to the male disciples.

*Only now* does Luke announce, "It was Mary Magdalene, Joanna, Mary the mother of James, and the other women with them who told this to the apostles" (24:10). Luke does not name them at the cross; Luke does not name them at the tomb. They only appear as individuals when they are reporting what they saw to the apostles. That very line tells me that for Luke, these women are *not* apostles. Luke doesn't even get around to naming a woman a "disciple" until Acts 9, when we meet Tabitha. Then again, as I've noted, the feminist in me has issues with Luke.

Luke's list of named women partially corresponds to the notice, which we've seen, that as Jesus proclaimed the kingdom of God throughout the Galilean villages, "some women who had been cured of evil spirits and infirmities: Mary, called Magdalene, from whom seven demons had gone out, and Joanna, the wife of Herod's steward Chuza, and Susanna, and many others, who provided for them out of their resources" (Luke 8:2-3).

These verses can suggest that the women, like the Twelve, were traveling with Jesus from place to place. I had for a number of years thought that to be the case, but my doubts are increasing. It seems to me unlikely that a group of women, let alone married women like Joanna, were overnighting in tents on the hillside or inns in the local towns, together with the male disciples, who themselves had left their wives and children at home. Had that happened, it's weird (at best) that Jesus is never accused of sexual infidelities. His opponents suggest he is possessed by Satan, playing on Satan's team, insane, a glutton and a drunkard, a blasphemer, and an anti-Roman agitator, but no one accuses him of sexual impropriety. Nor do we readers, contrary to the common view, ever actually see him in the company of prostitutes (unless we want to include prostitutes in the company of "sinners and tax collectors" with whom he is dining). The Gospels explicitly connect prostitutes along with tax collectors in the company of John the Baptizer (Matthew 21:32), but they are silent on prostitutes among Jesus's entourage.

It seems to me more likely that these women accompanied Jesus during the day and then returned to their homes at night. Their role was known throughout the Roman world as one of patronage: people with resources provide support for teachers and healers. For example, according to Josephus, Pharisees had women patrons (*Jewish Antiquities* 17.41-42); Lydia served as Paul's patron (Acts 16), and Tabitha (also known as Dorcas) in Joppa (Acts 9) served as patron to a group of widows.

The women of Luke 8 are not part of the inner circle of the Twelve, but they are faithful members of the movement. Luke may be encouraging women who read the Gospel to act as these women did, and so to contribute financially to the upkeep of the community without seeking leadership roles. It is these women who, together with the male followers, stand witness at the cross.

Luke also explains a major reason for the support the women provide Jesus: he had healed their bodies. The irony: Jesus restored them to health and to ritual purity, but they cannot do the same for him. The most they think they can do is honor his body by anointing it. But in Luke's account, unlike that of Mark, they are not redundant. Luke does not repeat the scene in Mark and Matthew where a woman anoints Jesus for his burial at the start of Holy Week. Luke transposes the scene to chapter 7, prior to Jesus's journey to Jerusalem; in Luke's version, a woman anoints Jesus's feet, not in relation to his burial but in gratitude for his forgiving her sins.

Finally, Luke adds that when the women shared their witness of what they experienced at the tomb with the male disciples, the men are not quick on the uptake. To the contrary, "these words seemed to them an idle tale, and they did not believe them" (Luke 24:11). At this point, commentators rush to explain this reaction by insisting that according to Jewish law, women's witness was not accepted. Thus, the apostles are following Jewish law in dismissing the women's testimony. Nonsense! First, the setting is not a law court, so a juridical explanation is irrelevant. In John's Gospel, Jesus's mother tells him the wine has run out; he doesn't say, "Your testimony is unacceptable." Mary Magdalene reports to Peter and the Beloved Disciple that the tomb is empty; they don't dismiss her claim on legal or any other grounds. Second, while Josephus proposes that the testimony of women in legal cases should not be accepted (*Jewish Antiquities* 4.219), his point is a proposition, a prescription, not a description of either past or present practices.

Third, no verse in the Tanakh (the Old Testament) forbids women's witness. To the contrary, women convey information frequently: if they did not, then the books of Ruth and Esther, the word of the prophet Deborah and the wise women of Abel Beth-Maacah and Tekoa would be discounted, and so on. Fourth, we see from John's Gospel that the issue is not the witnesses; the issue is the message itself. "Doubting" Thomas hears the proclamation of Jesus's resurrection from his fellow male disciples, but he only believes when he gets a personal appearance from Jesus himself. There's a second-century Christian text, known as the Epistle to the Apostles (the title could be a tongue twister) in which the male disciples not only fail to accept the proclamation of the women, but they also reject the proclamation from Jesus himself! Only when Jesus allows them to touch him do they accept that he has been raised. The problem in Luke 24:11 is not women witnesses and not Jewish law; it is the content of their message. If you've ever heard a message of something you thought was "unbelievable" and the message turned out to be true, you've come just a bit closer to the reaction of Luke's apostles.

## The Mother of Jesus and the Other Women in John's Version

John's description of the women at the cross does not have them looking on from a distance. To the contrary, John sets at the foot of the cross three or four women, but he only names two: "his mother, and his mother's sister, Mary the wife of Clopas, and Mary Magdalene" (John 19:25). The sister could be "Mary the wife of Clopas," or she could be "Salome" from Mark, and/or the mother of the sons of Zebedee from Matthew. A few people connect Clopas with Cleopas, one of the two followers who encounter Jesus on the road to Emmaus (see Luke 24:18), but the two names are distinct.

I'd prefer to think of "his mother's sister" as an unnamed sister. Thus, she could be any member of the group who called themselves "brothers" and "sisters"—a tradition carried on in some churches to this day. As the title "mother" features one role, the title "sister" includes another: the sister is known for her loyalty primarily to her sibling. When the mother of Jesus watches her son die on the cross, her sister is there to support her. That is what sisters are supposed to do.

## The Mother of Jesus

According to Mark 3:21, the family of Jesus, hearing the rumor that "he has gone out of his mind," went to "to restrain him." Jesus has been battling demons, for that is what exorcism is. That's a dangerous task, for demons—we might think of whatever keeps us from God, or goodness, health or family, life abundant or doing the right thing—have power. They can be seductive, or contagious. At this point in Mark, the scribes suggest that Jesus is in cahoots with Satan, and Jesus responds that a house divided against itself cannot stand (Mark 3:25). That's Jesus, not Shakespeare. It is also, by the way, the title of the speech Abraham Lincoln gave to his fellow Republicans on June 16, 1858, two and a half years before the outbreak of the Civil War.

Jesus's family, according to Mark, feared for his safety and his sanity. I think they were also a bit concerned for their own reputation. Since Mark has no annunciation to Mary, no angel telling her that she will bear the Son of God, and no quote from Isaiah about a virgin conceiving, there is no literary reason to think that the family has any clue about Jesus's messianic identity. He's Mary's son, and Mary, his mother, is worried about him.

Jesus has other concerns. When he is told just a few verses later, "Your mother and your brothers and sisters [yes, sisters!] are outside, asking for you" (Mark 3:32b), he responds, "'Who are my mother and my brothers?' And looking at those who sat around him, he said, 'Here are my mother and my brothers! Whoever does the will of God is my brother and sister and mother'" (Mark 3:33-35). The family of faith replaces the natal family. Unless Mark has hinted that Mary is at the cross, we would never know from Mark's narrative if she joined the movement. Then again, Mark 16:8 may be the end of the text, but it is by no means the end of the story.

Mary's story continues to develop in the Gospels. Matthew insists on the virginal conception through messages Joseph receives from an angel in dreams; Luke gives us Gabriel's annunciation to Mary as well as Mary's presence among the followers in Jerusalem after the death of her son. John locates the mother of Jesus as with him from Cana to cross. Later tradition has Mary at the Deposition, and her story will continue through the generations. In all these cases, we have choices on how to understand her. For example, do we focus on her biological status, on her fidelity, on the pathos of the mother at the cross, on her humility, or on her agency?

Only in John is the mother of Jesus explicitly at the cross, not at a distance but close enough to hear Jesus speak with her. That John does not name Jesus's mother "Mary" but identifies her as the "mother of Jesus" and that John consistently has Jesus refer to her as "woman" offer several points for theological assessment.

First, calling Mary "the mother of Jesus" provides a partial response to the emphasis on "Father" language in the Gospel of John. While the Fourth Gospel does not have the prayer that begins "Our Father…" it contains more appearances of the word *Father* than in the Synoptics. To refer to Mary as "the mother of Jesus" insists on his fully human embeddedness, in biology and in relationship.

Second, John 19:26 reads, "When Jesus saw his mother and the disciple whom he loved standing beside her…" The mother holds the primary position. The Beloved Disciple is for the moment off to the side. The word *mother* here is replete with all those other references to her, all in her maternal role. It is as a mother that she speaks to him at Cana, and she like a mother doesn't bother to fuss at his "woman" language because she knows what she wants him to do. The word *mother* has numerous, perhaps countless, connotations; we can understand the mother of Jesus, and so his relationship with her, with all those nuances.

Third, John's narrative shows that the maternal role need not be connected to biology. "When Jesus saw his mother and the Disciple whom he loved standing beside her, he said to his mother, 'Woman, here is your son'" (John 19:26). Jesus entrusts his mother to the Beloved Disciple and the Beloved Disciple to his mother. The disciple will support her, and she will support him. Their proximity at the cross will become their proximity for the future. But the mother retains her identity apart from being a mother, since she is still "woman." She takes on a new identity as the Beloved Disciple's adoptive mother. She participates in the new family Jesus has constructed: "Whoever does the will of God is my brother and sister and mother" (Mark 3:35). Reading this verse from Mark in light of John's Gospel, we can see another nuance. In the context of John, the will of God is the will of Jesus.

Finally, John tells us that "from that hour the disciple took her into his own home" (19:27b). Jesus had spoken about his hour. Now every hour can be sacred. We'll know when we enter those moments, as we will be displaying love.

Despite the youthful Mary whom Michelangelo depicts (one legend held that she always retained the face and body of a young woman), I suspect that when Jesus died, she was in her fifties. Jewish women at the time typically married in their late teens or early twenties (the idea that they married at twelve or thirteen comes from an incorrect reading of the Babylonian Talmud). Husbands were about ten years older. According to Luke's Gospel, "Jesus was about thirty years old when he began his work" (Luke 3:23a). That's possible, although Luke may be making a symbolic rather than historical point. Genesis 41:46 reports, "Joseph was thirty years old when he entered the service of Pharaoh king of Egypt"; according to 2 Samuel 5:4, "David was thirty years old when he began to reign, and he reigned forty years." The timing is conventional: men launched at thirty. In John's Gospel, there are a few hints that Jesus is older than thirty. In John 8:56, Jesus tells the Jews who are questioning him, "Your ancestor Abraham rejoiced that he would see my day; he saw it and was glad." The Jews, logically (it's hard to keep up with Jesus's language in John's Gospel) respond, "You are not yet fifty years old, and have you seen Abraham?" (John 8:57). Being "not yet fifty" is a good twenty years away from being thirty. Then again, I once asked my mother if she knew Abraham Lincoln. She did not. She was also not pleased with the question.

We might imagine the mother of Jesus with the standard symptoms of aging (I'm speaking personally here): a stiff back, arthritis in the fingers, deeper appreciation for naps. She can be fully independent, and yet her children and her younger friends feel the need to keep an eye on her. Or we can see her as strong, vigorous, just as capable as anyone else (yes, still speaking personally). I like to think that Jesus's plan for his mother would be a good guide for the Beloved Disciple: he needed her as much as she needed him. And if we identify the Beloved Disciple as John the son of Zebedee, then we can see the mother of Jesus finding companionship with Mrs. Zebedee, another mother who will know what it is like to lose a son.

## Calling Women "Woman"

From the cross, Jesus addresses his mother as "Woman." The address recollects several other scenes in the Gospel where Jesus calls other anonymous women "Woman." They are by no means all the same. We first meet the mother of Jesus not in the first chapter, for John has no Christmas story or infancy account. We meet her at the wedding at Cana, where in a major social gaff, the hosts have run out of wine. When the mother of Jesus mentions the problem to her son—clearly hinting that he ought to do something about it, and thus *she knows* he can do something about it—Jesus responds, "Woman, what concern is that to you and to me [literally: "what to me and to you"]? My hour has not yet come" (John 2:4). The mother, unperturbed at her son's abrupt response (and it is abrupt, even rude), advises the wine steward to do whatever Jesus tells him to do. Jesus is just being Jesus, and his mom knows her son. Now, at the cross, his hour has come.

The next time Jesus uses the address "Woman" occurs two chapters later, when Jesus says to the Samaritan at the well, "Woman, believe me, the hour is coming when you will worship the Father neither on this mountain nor in Jerusalem" (John 4:21). This second vocative "woman" and another reference to the hour signal pregnant (yes, I'm using the term deliberately) moments that connect the wine at Cana to the living water Jesus provides. They connect the biological mother with the multiply married Samaritan, of whom no mention of children is made. Insiders and outsiders are coming together.

The third use of the vocative "Woman" is from a passage that does not appear in the earlier manuscripts of John's Gospel, the account of the "woman taken in adultery" (John 8:1-10). From woman called "mother" but with no "father" present for Jesus except the one in heaven, to the Samaritan to whom Jesus states, "You have had five husbands, and the one you have now is not your husband" (John 4:18), to a woman who commits adultery, the Fourth Gospel has offered a fascinating array of sexual behavior. But in no case does Jesus condemn any of these women.

This familiar story in John 8 (and in some manuscripts in Luke—the story floats until it settles down in the Fourth Gospel) finds Jesus challenged by questioners who seek to trap him. They place before him a woman caught in the act of adultery and, to test him, ask, "In the law Moses commanded us to stone such women. Now what do you say?" (John 8:5). No one is about to stone her. They are not at a trial; there is no man accused with her. Rather, they want to catch him in a legal trap. If Jesus says, "Stone her," they will condemn him as too severe, for their tradition goes out of its way to avoid capital punishment; if he says, "Don't stone her," they can charge him with going against Torah without any community authority. Here is where, after writing on the ground (John shows that Jesus thus can both read and write), Jesus makes his famous comment about the one without sin casting the first stone.

The interlocutors leave, and Jesus is alone with the woman. He says to her, "Woman, where are they? Has no one condemned you?" (John 8:10). The woman answers, "No one, Lord" (or "sir"). Realizing that she is thinking of the interlocutors, Jesus makes clear that the "no one" includes him. "Neither do I condemn you. Go your way, and from now on do not sin again" (John 8:11). He does not forgive her—that would be a matter for her husband. But he does suggest she has a second chance.

After Jesus's address to his mother at the cross, the last appearance of the vocative "Woman" occurs in John 20:13. First, the angels at the tomb say to Mary Magdalene, "Woman, why are you weeping?" (John 20:13a); of course she's weeping (the angels' question seems a bit insensitive): she thinks someone has taken the body from the tomb. Then Jesus asks the same question, "Woman, why are you weeping?" (John 20:15). Mary thinks the man questioning her is the gardener; only when Jesus calls her by her name does she realize who is speaking with her.

Mary the single woman is identified by location (Magdala, a prosperous town in lower Galilee) rather than by maternal status, as a widow or as one multiply married or partnered out of wedlock or as one who committed adultery. Her reunion with Jesus—in a garden, with a case of mistaken identity and then a recognition scene, with the sense that she has been separated from the one whom she loves—these are all markers of the Hellenistic romance, contemporary popular novels of separated lovers. But just as Jesus does not marry the woman at the well (surprising in comparison to other "well" scenes: Rebecca meets Abraham's servant at a well, and she will marry Isaac, Rachel will marry Jacob, and Zipporah will marry Moses), so again he breaks convention by not going off with Mary Magdalene. Instead, he tells her to stop clinging to him and to proclaim his resurrection to the disciples. Much more can be, and should be said here, but that would move us from our topic of witnesses at the cross to witnesses at the resurrection. Moving on.

The mother of Jesus, the Samaritan woman, the woman caught in adultery, Mary Magdalene: Jesus calls them all "Woman" but at the same time recognizes their diversity, their gifts, and their needs. When Jesus addresses his mother as "Woman" at the cross, he is recollecting her appearance at Cana, and so he is guaranteeing her that all needs will be fulfilled. That massive amount of good wine at the wedding anticipates both Jesus's comments "Those who eat my flesh and drink my blood have eternal life, and I will raise them up on the last day.... Those who eat my flesh and drink my blood abide in me, and I in them" (John 6:54, 56) and his proclamation that *he* is the "true vine" (John 15:1). The vocative "Woman" also reminds us of the Samaritan woman and the role of living water. The two images come together at the cross, when (and this is only in the Fourth Gospel) "one of the soldiers pierced [Jesus's] side with a spear, and at once blood and water came out" (19:34). The stories of the women, addressed as "Woman," thus anticipate Baptism and Eucharist. And the address at the cross to his mother as "Woman" even recalls the address to the woman taken in adultery, who because of Jesus's intervention has a second change, a new life, a life abundant.

## And now?

John leaves us with one more allusion that influences our understanding of the women at the cross and in particular the "mother of Jesus." In his farewell discourses, Jesus notes, "When a woman is in labor, she has pain, because her hour has come. But when her child is born, she no longer remembers the anguish because of the joy of having brought a human being into the world. So you have pain now; but I will see you again, and your hearts will rejoice, and no one will take your joy from you" (John 16:21-22).

Mary Magdalene, the mother of Jesus, and the other women in John's account witness Jesus die. They carry that pain, that anguish, that the death of a loved one prompts. But their hearts will rejoice because the cross is never the end of the story.

The women at the cross have been ignored or reduced to models of simple piety. These women risked their lives, for women also were executed by the state. Some risked their marriages or their relationships with their children. For the Gospels, as well as for Israel's Scriptures, women are mothers, but they are also much more. Joanna, Mary Magdalene, Salome—none is identified as a mother. The Bible celebrates marriage and childbirth, but it also celebrates women's religious devotion, patronage, pilgrimage, witness, and a host of other matters not determined by marital status, gender, or sexuality. When Jesus states, "Woman!" he is not restricting his conversation partner to a gender role; he is making sure she is noticed.

## Chapter 6

# JOSEPH OF ARIMATHEA AND NICODEMUS

Joseph of Arimathea, the Sanhedrin member who gains Pilate's permission to take Jesus's body from the cross, shroud it, and place it in the tomb he owns in Jerusalem, appears in all four Gospels. Nicodemus, who comes to Jesus by night and learns about being born "from anew" or "from above" (not "born again"), who defends him against the chief priest, and who assists in the entombment, is present only in the Gospel of John. Together, the men help us think through several difficult issues, including sorting history from theology, the struggle between discipleship and social capital, the importance of showing respect for corpses, and the role of a sympathizer who cannot fully commit to joining the movement.

## Increasing Historical Details, Ancient Spin Control, or a Bit of Both?

*When evening had come, and since it was the day of Preparation, that is, the day before the sabbath, Joseph of Arimathea, a respected member of the council, who was also himself waiting expectantly for the kingdom of God, went boldly to Pilate and asked for the body of Jesus. Then Pilate wondered [the Greek literally means "marveled"] if he were*

*already dead; and summoning the centurion, he asked him*
*whether he had been dead for some time. When he learned*
*from the centurion that he was dead, he granted the body*
*[the Greek uses "corpse"] to Joseph. Then Joseph bought a*
*linen cloth, and taking down the body, wrapped it in the*
*linen cloth, and laid it in a tomb that had been hewn out of*
*the rock. He then rolled a stone against the door of the tomb.*

*Mark 15:42-46*

That's it. That's all we get from Mark's Gospel. Nothing about
when or where or even if Joseph had encountered Jesus other than
at the Council meeting. Nothing about Joseph's being a supporter
of Jesus or a disciple. To the contrary, Mark tells us that "the chief
priests and the whole council were looking for testimony against
Jesus to put him to death" (Mark 14:55). When the high priest
Caiaphas asked Jesus, "Are you the Messiah [Greek: *christos*], the
Son of the Blessed One?" Jesus replied, "I am" (Mark 14:61b-62a).
The priest proclaims this statement "blasphemy" (Mark 14:64). It
wasn't. Nevertheless, "All of them condemned him as deserving
death" (Mark 14:64).

In Mark's account, Joseph is a Sanhedrin member. He votes
to condemn Jesus, and then he takes the political risk of asking
Pilate for the body? Weird. And the story becomes stranger still.
The NRSV states that he "went boldly to Pilate and asked for
the body of Jesus" (Mark 15:43). The Greek term translated as
"boldly" has even stronger connotations; it could equally well be
translated "rashly" or "daringly." Paul uses the term in Philippians
1:14 to talk about his ministry while in captivity: "and most of the
brothers and sisters, having been made confident in the Lord by
my imprisonment, *dare* to speak the word [of God] with greater
boldness and without fear" (emphasis added). To wait for the
kingdom means, when the time comes, also to act—despite the
likelihood of negative effects. Joseph is one gutsy individual.

That Pilate released the "corpse" (the Greek term shifts from Joseph's request of the "body" to Pilate's releasing the "corpse") suggests not only that he regarded Jesus as innocent but also that he had no reason to worry about Jesus's followers. He did not anticipate whether the tomb would become a rallying site for revolution. We can speculate about Pilate's other motives: Did he feel guilty for condemning an innocent man? Did he see the proper burial as a fitting snub against Caiaphas the high priest who wanted to get Jesus out of the way? Was he being benevolent (which, at least according to the histories provided by Josephus and Philo, would be out of character)? Or might Mark be being ironic, for Mark chooses words carefully: Pilate "marvels," not at Jesus's teaching (see Mark 1:22) or his exorcisms (see Mark 5:20), his walking on water or his raising the dead, but that he died quickly. There have been and will be many more moments worthy of Pilate's marvel, and ours.

According to Mark 15:45, Pilate granted not the body but the "corpse" of Jesus to Joseph. Again, words matter. The only other time the Gospel uses the word "corpse" is in reference to the decapitated corpse of John the Baptizer: "When his disciples heard about [his death], they came and took his body [Greek: "corpse"], and laid it in a tomb" (Mark 6:29). The cluster of similar concerns—a man of God executed by the ruling authorities, the disposition of the corpse, the tomb—makes the pathos of Jesus's death even stronger: while John is buried by his disciples, according to Mark, Jesus is buried by a stranger, one who at least according to Mark voted for his execution. As for Jesus's disciples, Mark reports, "All of them deserted him and fled" (Mark 14:50).

The strangeness of Joseph's actions continues. We know that Jesus has family: his mother appears at the cross in John's Gospel, and his brother James will eventually become the leader of the Jerusalem community gathered in Jesus's name. However, Mark gives no indication that members of Jesus's family numbered among his followers, and as we saw in the last chapter, it is not clear that Mark locates Mary the mother of Jesus at either cross or tomb. Where are the relatives to care for the body?

Even weirder, in Mark's account, Joseph entombs Jesus without any mourning or funeral rites. No anointing the body; no prayers. He could have waited; indeed, rabbinic tradition would have allowed him to do so. Or he could have planned: given that he had enough time to get to Pilate and then get back to Golgotha, he would also have had enough time to send someone to pick up the spices. On the other hand, as we saw in the previous chapter, Jesus had already been anointed for his burial by an anonymous woman several days earlier.

Mark's description of Joseph of Arimathea is both historically plausible and theologically instructive. On the matter of history: Rome sometimes permitted friends and family members to claim the corpse of the victim of state-sanctioned capital punishment. Philo, the Jewish philosopher from Alexandria, wrote a treatise known as *Against Flaccus*, in which he speaks of a pogrom instigated by Flaccus, the Roman prefect of Egypt, against the Jews in Alexandria in 38 CE (he did not date the text "38 CE," but you know what I mean). In this work, Philo observes,

> I have known instances before now of men who had been crucified when this festival and holiday [the emperor's birthday] was at hand, being taken down and given up to their relations, in order to receive the honours of sepulture, and to enjoy such observances as are due to the dead; for it used to be considered, that even the dead ought to derive some enjoyment from the natal festival of a good emperor, and also that the sacred character of the festival ought to be regarded. (*Flaccus* 83).

In other words, corpses of people executed by the state could be returned to friends and family as part of the celebration of the emperor's birthday. What a benevolent governmental system (yes, I'm being facetious).

Not only Philo but also archaeology indicates that victims of crucifixion did receive, on occasion, a proper burial. In 1968, at Givat Hamivtar, in East Jerusalem, which is the site of several ancient tombs, archaeologists discovered in an ossuary (bone box) the remains of a man named Jehohanan [Jonathan] ben [son of] H'galqol; the remains included a right heel bone pierced with a 7-inch-long iron nail. Archaeologists also noted that nails had also been driven through the man's wrists.

Finally, that a fellow from Arimathea owned a plot in Jerusalem is also historically plausible. We are not sure where Arimathea is; the reference could be to Ramathaim-Zophim, in the hill country of Ephraim; the location, about twenty miles north of Jerusalem, is the home of Elkanah and Hannah, the parents of the prophet Samuel (1 Samuel 1:1). The name could simply indicate Joseph's hometown, or it could be an allusion to Samuel, the prophet who anointed King David. As Samuel anointed David, so Joseph will metaphorically anoint the body of Jesus with spices (as in John's Gospel). This connection strikes me as a stretch. Or, for another stretch, we can play with the name in terms of etymology. The Greek word *aristos* means "best" or "glorious," as in "aristocrat" and even the name "Aristotle." As for the *mathea* part of Arimathea: the Greek term for disciple is *mathetes*. Thus, Arimathea can signal "best disciple." The name Joseph comes from the Hebrew root meaning "to add" (we see the punning basis of the name in Genesis 30:24, Rachel "named him Joseph, saying, 'May the LORD add to me another son!'" Thus, we have "added the best disciple." Meh.

As for a man from Arimathea owning a burial plot in Jerusalem, that makes good sense. To be buried in Jerusalem, the "holy city," would be a sign of reverence, but it could also be a sign of some economic security. The same is true today; some people can afford cemetery plots or a place in a columbarium; others are interred in a "potter's field"—the name comes from Matthew 27:6-10, and it concerns the thirty pieces of silver that Judas returned to the priests. The priests do not want to keep blood money in the Temple, so they used it "to buy the potter's field as a place to bury foreigners." Matthew adds, "Then was fulfilled what had been spoken through the prophet Jeremiah, 'And they took the thirty pieces of silver, the price of the one on whom a price had been set...and they gave them for the potter's field, as the Lord commanded me'" (Matthew 27:9-10). The citation is a conflation of Zechariah 11:12-13, Jeremiah 18:1-19, and Jeremiah 32:6-15.

It is Matthew who tells us that the tomb was Joseph's own (Matthew 27:60). Perhaps he thought his body would lie in repose next to that of Jesus; perhaps Joseph anticipated that his bones would be collected in an ossuary with those of Jesus. If so, he was mistaken. Joseph may have thought about connection to Jesus in death; to the contrary, Jesus proclaimed that God is the "God of the living" (Matthew 22:32 // Mark 12:27 // Luke 20:38).

And yet, we might stop to think about such matters. Where do we want to be? My parents are buried next to each other in the same cemetery in New Bedford, Massachusetts, where four generations of my family rest ("rest" is an interesting metaphor). Once a year I try to visit the cemetery, to put stones on my parents' grave—a single headstone—as Jews mark the visiting of a cemetery. Flowers die; rocks are permanent. Do we want our families and friends to be able to "visit" us? How do we want to be remembered, and what do we want our epitaphs to proclaim?

Along with history, the report about Joseph has theological resonances. Underlying Mark's description may well be the fourth of Isaiah's so-called "suffering servant" songs. One viable translation of Isaiah 53:9 is "They made his grave with the wicked / and his tomb with the rich." Mark may have presumed that a member of the Council, who had access to the Roman governor, would be both rich and wicked. Matthew, always happy to show how Jesus "fulfilled" prophecy, makes the point about Joseph's income explicit, as we'll see below.

The concern for fulfillment of this prophecy may lie behind a fifth account, along with the canonical Gospels of the deposition and then the entombment. In this version, neither Joseph nor Nicodemus appears. In a speech to the people in a synagogue in Psidian Antioch (that is, southern Turkey), Paul states:

> Because the residents of Jerusalem and their leaders did not recognize him or understand the words of the prophets that are read every sabbath, they fulfilled those words by condemning him. Even though they found no cause for a sentence of death, they asked Pilate to have him killed. When they had carried out everything that was written about him, they took him down from the tree and laid him in a tomb.
>
> Acts 13:27-29

For this speech, composed by Luke and placed on Paul's lips, the responsibility for Jesus's condemnation, death, and burial all resides with the Jewish "residents of Jerusalem" who misunderstood their own scriptures (even though no one, prior to the life and death of Jesus, was expecting a crucified messiah). These people were at the cross and they put the corpse in the tomb. In Paul's speech, Rome's involvement in the Crucifixion goes missing. Joseph of Arimathea goes missing as well. And with this absence come more questions of history. Luke knows the story of Rome's involvement; Luke knows the story of Joseph of Arimathea. Has Luke tailored Paul's talk for a Jewish audience? Does our audience change how we tell our stories?

Questions continue past history to ethics: Can an outsider, as Joseph is at least in Mark's Gospel, still do the right thing? Could a person cast a vote for a bill we think is immoral but turn around and act in a fully moral manner to people impacted by that bill? Can we judge a person guilty but still recognize the humanity of that individual (you might hear again my concern for my insider students at Riverbend)? Do we, as readers, know what was in Joseph's mind as he cast his guilty vote? As he took the body from the cross?

Finally, it is unlikely that Joseph took the body and entombed it on his own. He had to have had help. Unmentioned and so unnoticed are the servants or slaves who carried the body; unmentioned and unnoticed are the people who rolled the stone from the tomb and then sealed it. There were others involved in Jesus's burial, and their names are lost to history. What did they think? Had we been witnesses to the trial and then Jesus's death, and to his entombment, what would we think?

## Retelling the Story

Matthew 27:57 adds two details to Mark's account. "When it was evening, there came a *rich man* from Arimathea, named Joseph, who was also *a disciple* of Jesus" (emphasis added). The first part of this addition states the obvious: since Joseph owns a tomb in Jerusalem, he is rich. Most people were buried in trenches dug into the ground. The only other time Matthew uses the term "rich" is in relation to the saying about how it is easier for a camel to go through the eye of a needle than it is for a rich person to enter the kingdom of heaven (Matthew 19:23-24). But rich people can nevertheless be disciples if they use their funds to help others. I am reminded here also of the magi, who appear in Matthew's Christmas story. Jesus is greeted by rich benefactors at his birth, and he is attended by a rich benefactor at his death.

Matthew's second point, that Joseph is a "disciple," is less obvious, especially since he had been part of that condemning

Sanhedrin. Nor had he been mentioned before in the Gospel. Last we had any reference to the disciples was at Jesus's arrest, when Matthew reports, "Then all the disciples deserted him and fled" (Matthew 26:56). Had I been Matthew's editor, I would have suggested he write, "Then the eleven remaining disciples in the insider-group deserted him," although that does sound clunky. Were Joseph a member of the Sanhedrin that condemned Jesus, then he would be even more a failure than Peter, who denied his Lord three times while the Sanhedrin was sitting in judgment. To condemn Jesus, to mock him and strike him, sounds worse than to deny him. I have a suspicion that Joseph was not a disciple, and that Matthew is engaging in spin control. For readers, perhaps especially well-off readers, knowing that Jesus had disciples among the upper classes might entice them to learn more.

Luke provides even more detail, and Joseph continues to look better and better: "Now there was a good and righteous man named Joseph, who, though a member of the council, had not agreed to their plan and action. He came from the Jewish town of Arimathea, and he was waiting expectantly for the kingdom of God" (Luke 23:50-51). In Luke's account, Joseph did not fail in his discipleship. He did not agree to condemn Jesus. He was righteous, the same term the centurion at the cross in Luke's Gospel uses to describe Jesus. I do wonder how Luke imagines the trial: Did Joseph speak up? Did he vote no? Did he abstain, and if he did, is he showing righteousness, or cowardice?

Luke agrees with Mark that Joseph "took [the corpse] down, wrapped it in a linen cloth, and laid it in a rock-hewn tomb where no one had ever been laid" (Luke 23:53). Luke does not, however, identify Joseph as a "rich" man because people who are so identified in Luke, usually in parables, are negative rather than positive exemplars (see, for example, the Parable of the Rich Man and Lazarus in Luke 16:19-31; see also Luke 12:16; 16:1). The only good "rich" man so identified for Luke is Zacchaeus the tax collector (Luke 19:2).

John adds even more detail, and at this point, Joseph has gone from the ambivalent figure in Mark to the premier disciple: "Joseph of Arimathea, who was a disciple of Jesus, though a secret one because of his fear of the Jews, asked Pilate to let him take away the body of Jesus. Pilate gave him permission; so he came and removed his body" (John 19:38). Nothing here about Joseph's participation in the Sanhedrin trial, for there is no Sanhedrin trial in John's Gospel; there is only a hearing before Annas, Caiaphas's father-in-law and the previous high priest (John 18:13, 24). By the time we get to John's Gospel, Joseph becomes fully exonerated from any complicity in condemning Jesus.

He is also here detached from his Jewish identity. The comment "his fear of the Jews" is the Fourth Gospel's way of signaling the division between the broader Jewish community and the followers of Jesus. It's an odd phrase, given that Joseph (as well as Jesus!) are also Jews. This line echoes John's notice of the Jewish people's confusion regarding Jesus earlier on: "While some were saying, 'He is a good man,' others were saying, 'No, he is deceiving the crowd.' Yet no one would speak openly about him for fear of the Jews" (John 7:12-13). This distancing language that separates Jesus and his followers from their fellow Jews also anticipates Jesus's post-resurrection encounter with his disciples: "When it was evening on that day, the first day of the week, and the doors of the house where the disciples had met were locked for fear of the Jews, Jesus came and stood among them and said, 'Peace be with you'" (John 20:19). When we read John's Gospel, we need to be careful lest we vilify Jesus's own people.

Although John does eliminate the Sanhedrin trial, he does add another member of the Council to the story, and so we turn to Nicodemus, one of the New Testament's most puzzling, and intriguing, figures.

## Nicodemus the Pharisee

Nicodemus, mentioned only in the Gospel of John, would be an odd person for the Synoptic Gospels to ignore. In the Fourth Gospel, Nicodemus helps Joseph of Arimathea prepare the body of Jesus and bury it; he also has a personal audience with Jesus and later defends him against his accusers. While his absence from the Synoptics makes me worry about his historicity, I find him a fascinating, complex character.

His name can be symbolic: *Nico*, which is the same term as the athletic brand Nike, means "victory"; *demus*, from the root that gives us terms like both *democracy* and *demagogue*, means "people." Etymologically, *Nicodemus* means "Conqueror of the people" or "Victory over the people." It's an optimistic name for parents to give a child. It is also ironic in John's Gospel. Whereas John introduces him as "There was a Pharisee named Nicodemus, a leader of the Jews" (John 3:1), Jesus undercuts his role: "Are you a teacher of Israel, and yet you do not understand these things?" (John 3:10). The conqueror has been conquered.

On the other hand, the name also appears in both Greek and Hebrew texts, all connected to the same multigenerational family. According to our first-century Jewish historian Josephus (*Jewish War* 2.451; *Jewish Antiquities* 14.37), members of a prominent, wealthy family associated with the name Nicodemus attempted to stop the first revolt against the Romans. According to the Babylonian Talmud (Gittin 56a; the tradition appears in other late rabbinic texts as well), Naqdimon (i.e., Nicodemus) ben Gurion and two other wealthy men from Jerusalem promised the emperor Vespasian that they would provide the people of Jerusalem wheat and barley, wine, oil, salt, and wood, during the Roman siege. According to b. Ta'anit 19b-20, Naqdimon sought to purchase water for pilgrims coming to the Jerusalem Temple. Should he not be able to repay in water, he would give the Gentile with whom he made the contract "twelve talents of silver" (that's a lot of silver). A year goes by. No rain. On the day the debt is due, the Gentile asks for the silver. Naqdimon goes the Temple and prays, "I do this not for my honor but for yours, so that the pilgrims would have water." God hears the prayer, and the rain falls.

It could happen.

Never ones to let a good story end (much like the chapters in the Gospel of John), the Talmud continues by having the Gentile agree that while it did rain, not enough fell by the end of the day to make up for the debt. Thus, the debt still stands. Naqdimon goes back into the Temple that night and prays. Suddenly, the clouds part and the sun shines. Hence the name Naqdimon, which the rabbis read as a pun on the Aramaic word *nikdera*, meaning "the sun has broken through" (it's one way of dealing with an obviously Greek name). If this whole scenario sounds far-fetched, you might have a look at Joshua 10:12-13 (cf. Sirach 46:4) where, we read, the sun stood still. (At this point, I feel compelled to state that neither Joshua 10 nor the Talmudic passage in question should be read as promoting scientific fact.)

There are other Talmudic stories of Naqdimon, including one legend of his fabulously wealthy daughter Miriam, who lost all her possessions in the first revolt against Rome. More intriguing, in the Talmud, Naqdimon is also known by the name Buni, and elsewhere in the Talmud, Buni is the name of one of Jesus's disciples. Just as astounding, the Talmud (b. Sanhedrin 43a) identifies another of Jesus's disciples by the name Nakkai, which looks and sounds like an abbreviation of Naqdimon. Perhaps the authors of these Talmudic passages had heard of Nicodemus, the disciple of Jesus. At times, later rabbinic sources can be used to shed light on the New Testament. At other times, the New Testament can provide background information on rabbinic texts. Thus, Jews and Christians need each other, historically, to fill in the gaps in our histories.

Back to John's account, where Nicodemus and Joseph accord the body of Jesus not only the customary honors but an extreme version of them: "Nicodemus, who had at first come to Jesus by night, also came, bringing a mixture of myrrh and aloes, weighing about a hundred pounds. They took the body of Jesus and wrapped it with the spices in linen cloths, according to the burial custom of the Jews" (John 19:39-40). The verse contradicts Mark, who depicts the women as coming to the cross to anoint the body (as we saw in the last chapter).

To help in interpreting this description, we backtrack to Nicodemus's two other appearances in the Gospel. Each time he fails to move past the "interested and even sympathetic observer" to disciple stage. We meet him first in chapter 3, where John introduces him as "a Pharisee named Nicodemus, a leader of the Jews" who comes to Jesus "by night" (John 3:1-2). He is both literally and figuratively in the dark. The Fourth Gospel plays with images of light and darkness: Jesus is the "light of all people" (John 1:4), the light that "shines in the darkness and the darkness did not overcome it" (1:5), the "light" to whom the Baptizer testifies (1:7-8), the "true light which enlightens everyone" (1:9), "the light [that] has come into the world" (3:19), the "light of the world" (8:12), and more. Nicodemus needs to get himself out of the dark. He never quite makes it.

Nicodemus approaches Jesus not because of his teaching but because of his "signs": "Rabbi," he says, "we know that you are a teacher who has come from God; for no one can do these signs that you do apart from the presence of God" (John 3:2). The only "sign" John has recounted thus far is Jesus's turning water into wine at Cana (2:1-10), and there is no evidence that Nicodemus, located in Jerusalem, was on the Cana guest list. However, John has noted that Jesus performed other signs in Jerusalem, at the time of the Passover holiday (2:23). For all the glorious signs Jesus does, these do not and should not serve as proof of his identity. Rather, they suggest a faith based on the wrong details. In John 4:48, Jesus castigates the royal official who had asked him to heal his son, "Unless you see signs and wonders you will not believe." The two "you" references are in the plural. Seeing signs might make people curious about Jesus, but signs should not be necessarily for belief. As Jesus says to "Doubting" Thomas, "Have you believed because you have seen me? Blessed are those who have not seen and yet have come to believe" (John 20:29).

The concern for signs that Nicodemus shares makes sense to me. I have had a number of both students and friends remark that the signs make them depressed rather than inspired: "Jesus raises Lazarus, so why did he not raise my mother?" or "Jesus provided wine for the wedding, so why does he not provide bread for my table?" or "The man born blind can now see, so why am I losing my sight?" Signs are the big show, but the good news may better, even best, be found in the small acts, or what today we call random acts of kindness: the person who sits by the dying friend in the hospice; the unsung individuals who work in food banks; the youth willing to read aloud to the sightless older person. These types of signs are all around. Signs in themselves tend to confirm what we are already inclined to believe: many religions depict their divinities or their prophets as producing signs, or miracles, or mighty works. Adherents of one tradition tend to accept the stories in their own tradition as "miracles" but dismiss the stories of other traditions as fake, as myth, or as magic rather than miracle. Nicodemus's opening line prompts the question: How do we assess a sign? How do we determine what the sign signifies?

In contrast to Nicodemus, whom we meet in chapter 3, the Samaritan woman in chapter 4 gets it from the beginning. John states that Jesus came to the well "about noon" (John 4:6), and it was then he met a woman from Samaria. High noon—*of course* she gets it. "Come and see," she says, "a man who told me every-thing I have ever done. He cannot be the Messiah, can he?" (John 4:29). With this line, she becomes the Gospel's first successful evangelist. When Mary Magdalene comes to Jesus's tomb "early on the first day of the week, while it was still dark" (John 20:1), attentive readers know that she will soon be walking in the light, and with the light.

Nicodemus, in the night, and in the dark, is not a disciple. Nevertheless, he makes very good points. He recognizes Jesus as a "teacher who has come from God" (John 3:2), and he asks what Jesus is talking about (3:9), for in John's Gospel especially, Jesus is not always clear. In turn, Jesus does not toss Nicodemus out; rather, he attempts to instruct him about the need to be born "anew" or "from above" by water and Spirit. The same Greek term that can be translated "anew" or "from above" can also mean "again," and that's how Nicodemus understands Jesus: "Can one enter a second time into the mother's womb and be born?" he asks (John 3:4). Hence, the expression "born-again Christian" is not what Jesus had in mind. This scene in John, by the way, is a very early example of the humor that comes when people misunderstand a word that has more than one definition. I look at John 3 as an early incarnation of the famous Abbott and Costello routine, "Who's on First." (If you've never heard this, take the time to listen.) But I digress.

Jesus even grants to Nicodemus the Fourth Gospel's most famous line, "For God so loved the world that he gave his only Son, so that everyone who believes in him may not perish but may have eternal life" (John 3:16). Jesus is not, to quote from the Sermon on the Mount, casting pearls before swine. He is, to mix a metaphor, doing his best to plant the seed of faith in Nicodemus.

More, Jesus hints to Nicodemus about his impending death as well as his return to the Father: "Just as Moses lifted up the serpent in the wilderness, so must the Son of Man be lifted up" (John 3:14). Jesus is referring to one of the Bible's more enigmatic scenes (which is saying something). As Numbers 21 recounts, the Israelites, wandering for forty years between enslavement in Egypt and freedom in the Promised Land, start (again) to grumble. They complain to both God and Moses, "Why have you brought us up out of Egypt to die in the wilderness? For there is no food and no water, and we detest this miserable food" (Numbers 21:5). The irony of the complaint is delicious: either there is no food, or there is plenty of food, but it doesn't taste good.

God, not one to appreciate the humor, sends a plague of poisonous serpents. Moses then makes "a serpent of bronze"; he "put it upon a pole, and whenever a serpent bit someone, that person would look at the serpent of bronze and live" (Numbers 21:9). This practice represents what anthropologists call "apotropaic magic." It works somewhat like homeopathy, for an apotropaic image is a symbol of evil that wards off evil. Gargoyles and jack-o'-lanterns fit into this category. So in part does the image of the cross: the symbol of death becomes the symbol of life. According to 2 Kings 18:4, the good king Hezekiah "broke in pieces the bronze serpent that Moses had made" because the people were worshipping it. Apotropaic images can become fetish objects; items made to do good can become idols or traps or obsessions. The entire discussion sends us back to the cross, the instrument of torture on which Jesus died. When we see a cross, or a crucifix, what thoughts do we have?

When John's Gospel speaks of Jesus being "lifted up," the reference is both to his being crucified and to his being exalted. Once again, the Fourth Gospel plays with words. Nicodemus, who tends to remain on the literal rather than the metaphorical or allegorical level of language, does not recognize the import of Jesus's reference to the serpent, but the well-informed reader should. So does the well-informed art historian. Starting in the eleventh century, Christian artists began to depict the crucified Christ in the shape of the letter s, with his knees bent to the side. Thus, his body takes the form of a snake to remind viewers of that ancient bronze snake that saved ancient Israel.

We meet Nicodemus a second time in John 7, where he defends Jesus against the accusations of his fellow Pharisees. His defense is based not on the value of Jesus's teaching but on legal precedent: "Nicodemus, who had gone to Jesus before, and who was one of them, asked, 'Our law does not judge people without first giving them a hearing to find out what they are doing, does it?'" (John 7:50-51). His legal argument results in derision when his fellow Pharisees tease him, "Surely you are not also from Galilee, are you? Search and you will see that no prophet is to arise from Galilee" (John 7:52). Both Nicodemus and his opponents argue from the same textual basis, the Scriptures of Israel, but they have different emphases. Nicodemus concentrates on what the Torah says; the Pharisees on what the Torah does not say. Nicodemus might have noted that absence of evidence is not the same thing as evidence of absence. Once again, Nicodemus does the right thing, and once again he does not become a disciple. I am liking him more and more.

Finally, we return to the cross. After introducing Joseph of Arimathea, John mentions "Nicodemus, who had first come to Jesus by night" (19:39). The night repetition reminds us that Nicodemus is still more-or-less walking in the dark. He will not be at the tomb at dawn, like Mary Magdalene, Peter, and the Beloved Disciple. But again, he does the right thing by providing Jesus an honorable burial and by working with the disciple (at least according to John's Gospel), Joseph of Arimathea.

For me, Nicodemus represents the sympathizer, the person who might attend the church services, or even serve on church committees, but who is not technically a member of the church. I have a very good friend who, although not a Presbyterian by birth or baptism, worships in a Presbyterian church because that is where his partner worships. Other friends, Roman Catholic to the core, have been worshipping via zoom at an Episcopal church because they find that the Episcopal priest there speaks to their concerns, and to their hearts, in a way that the priest in their own parish does not. In my synagogue in Nashville, we have many faithful participants—whether partnered with members, devoted to the congregation and its Torah study, or interested in Judaism, but some not willing to give up their Christian practices and beliefs and others are not interested in converting to Judaism. We in the congregation welcome them, enjoy their company, and are delighted that they want to spend time with us in worship.

Churches and synagogues have always had nonmember affiliates. In antiquity, Gentiles who participated in synagogue activities were, as we've seen in our discussion of the centurion, known as "God-fearers"; some, such as Cornelius the centurion in Acts 10, even appear in the New Testament.

Perhaps at some point these God-fearers will convert; perhaps not. Our job, as members of the congregation, is to support them, to answer their questions as best as we can, to avoid pressuring them to choose one tradition over another, and to learn from them how our tradition might sound to one who is not a member. The Nicodemuses (Nicodemi? Nicodemoi? Nicodemim? I do not know the appropriate plural) in our midst are to be welcomed, cherished, and treated with love, as we are commanded to "love the stranger who dwells among us" (cf. Leviticus 19:34).

## History and/or Theology?

These brief accounts of Joseph of Arimathea along with John's several mentions of Nicodemus leave us with several questions of historicity. I mention them since to ignore them would be academically irresponsible. I don't appreciate biblical studies that avoid the hard questions, whether of history or theology; I have known too many students who are shaken to their core in biblical studies classes when they suddenly realize that there are contradictions in the Bible. Their earlier teachers, or the clergy, should have alerted them to the differences. Biblical studies, in my view, should support belief when belief is already present, rather than destroy it. Nor do I think that concluding a biblical passage might be more spin control than fact, or parable rather than history, is necessarily a bad thing. We are not talking about "alternative facts"; we are talking about how the Bible is designed, like a sermon or a parable, to encourage people in their faith journey. Not everything needs to have happened, in the sense of being caught on a camera, in order to be meaningful.

In the same way I do not appreciate approaches to the Bible that refuse to acknowledge questions of history, I also find distasteful the type of biblical study in which faculty adduce distinct stories or questions of historicity to discount the Bible or to undermine someone's belief. That is no more appropriate than the fundamentalist literalist reading that would discount literary artistry and/or scientific fact. Distinctions and matters of history should serve as prompts to increase appreciation of the multiple messages the text can convey.

Some biblical scholars, including me, doubt the historicity of a full Sanhedrin trial on the first night of Passover, and thus I doubt that Joseph of Arimathea was at that trial. That all three Synoptic Gospels describe such a trial does not give us multiple witnesses. Matthew likely used Mark as a source, and Luke had access to Mark as well as, probably, to Matthew. Other factors also speak against historicity. For example, if the trial did take place, it operated in a manner contrary to both law and logic.

The Sanhedrin did not meet at night, and to have a meeting after the Passover seder, the meal celebrating the Exodus from Egypt, would have been a logistical nightmare (it would be like convening the entire Senate and the Supreme Court to sit in judgment on Christmas Eve, following the family dinner). Rabbinic texts, which, granted, postdate the New Testament and so may not be accurate witnesses to first-century procedures, go out of their way to ensure that capital cases do not end with execution: all of the numerous safeguards, including a forty-day search for witnesses to speak on behalf of the accused, go missing in the Synoptic accounts. Nor is Jesus guilty of anything. When Caiaphas states that Jesus had blasphemed by calling himself the "Messiah, the Son of the Blessed One" (Mark 14:62-63), he condemns Jesus on a false charge. Jesus did not blaspheme. It's too bad kangaroos are not indigenous to the Middle East, or the term "kangaroo court" would be even more apt.

The Gospel of John recounts not a full trial but only a hearing before Annas, Caiaphas's father-in-law and the former high priest. John also dates the Crucifixion to the day before the Passover, when the lambs for the meal are being sacrificed in the Temple. John's single hearing, and John's chronology, both make more historical sense.

Although I do not think that there was a Sanhedrin trial, the narrative nevertheless lends itself to numerous important questions. Let's imagine that the full Sanhedrin trial happened, and Joseph were present. He had options. He could have, as he does in John's version of the story, supported Jesus. So we realize how hard it is to be the one voice amid others who are so politically and ideologically driven that they want to execute someone. When I think of Joseph of Arimathea, I also think of Henry Fonda in the original (1953) filming of the teleplay *Twelve Angry Men*. How easy it is to go with the majority; how hard it is to stand up for justice; it is even harder to argue for it. The same problems continue today: politicians who know that a vote, just one vote, will cost them the next election; student government members who know that a vote, just one vote, might get them canceled. When do we give in to the majority, and when do we hold our ground? More, how do we distinguish what we believe from the actions of the group to which we belong, since we do not always side with every plank in the platforms of our political party, or religious institution, or social club?

Joseph had other options. He has access to Pilate, which suggests he's not only a respected individual but a socially prominent one. He could have stopped, or at least tried to stop, Pilate's judgment. Similarly, Nicodemus, a "leader of the Jews" (John 3:1), also had options: as a leader, he could have come to Jesus in the daylight rather than at night (John 3:2), or hosted Jesus at a dinner party to introduce him to other friendly Pharisees. We can always do more. And when we do not, and bad things happen, we may find ourselves with guilt. What then can we do to expiate it?

Everyone had options: people could have tried to stop the execution. They did not. Would we? We do not know the history behind Joseph of Arimathea or Nicodemus. But we do learn, so very much, from what the Gospel writers tell us about them.

# Joseph of Arimathea: Waiting Expectantly for the Kingdom of God (Mark 15:43)

Joseph anticipated the *kingdom* of God. In reading the Gospels, we should not separate the idea of this divine kingdom (Greek: *basileia*) from the "king" whom the Gospels portray, Jesus of Nazareth, son of David. For the Gospels, the king and the kingdom arrive together. In the presence of Jesus, one should be able to sense the kingdom, to touch it in the passing of the peace in a

church context, to taste it in the Eucharist, to hear it in the sing-
ing. But the church building is not the only place where people
both wait expectantly for the kingdom and sense its presence.

There are obvious places: where strangers are welcome, the
hungry are fed, the naked clothed. The notice to the sheep and
the goats has reached the conventional status: yes, we know all
this, even if we don't act on it. I suggest that to wait expectantly
for the kingdom is to act; waiting does not mean sitting back in the
recliner and watching the news.

Waiting for the bus to arrive or the lecture to end is one thing;
waiting for the kingdom is something else. To wait for the kingdom
and *not* to act on that desire is to fail to act in partnership with
God. Joseph of Arimathea waited, and he acted: in the court, with
Pilate, with the body of Jesus, at the cross and the tomb. If we wait
and we do not act when the hour comes, we will be out of time.

## Joseph and Discipleship

Joseph of Arimathea, who at least in Mark is not a disciple,
ironically models one of the signs of discipleship. Jesus told his
disciples: "You will stand before governors and kings because of
me, as a testimony to them" (Mark 13:9b). Joseph is the first
disciple to act as such, and he puts himself at risk in doing so.
Rome executed Jesus as "king of the Jews," a title meant to mock
both Jesus and the Jewish people. But kings have followers, so
Joseph, in asking the governor for the body of Jesus, risked being
taken as a follower of a man convicted of sedition. More, were
Joseph a member of the Sanhedrin, which according to Mark
not only unjustly convicted Jesus but harassed him as well, then
Joseph also risks ostracism from his own people. Nor does Joseph
of Arimathea think that Jesus is going to rise from the dead; if he
did, the boulder in front of the tomb—the one the women wonder
about how they will move it—is at best a disincentive to exiting. If
we read John's account, so is one hundred pounds of myrhh.

In claiming the body of Jesus and placing it in the tomb, Joseph of Arimathea has nothing to gain and everything to lose. How brilliant. He is the model of Jesus's comment, "For those who want to save their life will lose it, and those who lose their life for my sake, and for the sake of the gospel, will save it" (Mark 8:35).

## Caring for the Dead

The stories of Joseph and Nicodemus remind us of those who care for the bodies of the dead. The Jewish tradition mandates that the corpse should be washed, which could be part of the "burial custom" referenced in John 19:40: "They took the body of Jesus and wrapped it with the spices in linen cloths, according to the burial custom of the Jews." The washing would be especially appropriate in the case of a victim of scourging and then crucifixion. The Book of Acts gives us one of the earliest examples of this Jewish custom; according to Acts 9:37, after the disciple Tabitha (the only woman explicitly called a "disciple" in the New Testament!) had died, her friends "washed her" and then "laid her in a room upstairs." This attention to the corpse is so important that, according to the Mishnah (m. Shabbat 23:5), the commandment to wash the body overrides Sabbath observance.

I know that when my parents died, the *chevra kadisha* (literally, from the Aramaic, "holy fellowship"), the Jewish burial society in New Bedford watched over the bodies until the burial the day after they died. These dedicated men and women prepare the corpse by washing it and shrouding it. The custom, which has prevailed from early antiquity until today, gives solace to families and more, it also tends the bodies of individual Jews who may have no family. The motives of the people who participate in this ritual are entirely altruistic. Whereas obeying most of the mitzvot, the commandments, can have a positive outcome—if I love my neighbor as myself, that neighbor may reciprocate that love—

there is no possibility of reciprocation in burying a corpse. The corpse is not going to return the favor.

My Nashville synagogue's website reads, "The Nashville Chevra Kadisha is always here to help you in your time of need. From *tahara* (washing and dressing) to *shemira* (staying with the deceased and reciting Psalms), our members take care of everything from the time of death until after the funeral service" (http://www .sherithisrael.com/pages/shul-cemetery-chevra-kadisha).Joseph of Arimathea and Nicodemus remind us of the duty, and the privilege, of tending to a corpse. Such action honors the tradition, honors the individual who is in the image and likeness of the divine, provides comfort to the family, and provides solace to all Jews: we know that our bodies will not be dishonored.

## And Now?

Christian legend embellished the stories of both Joseph of Arimathea and Nicodemus. In one account, Joseph of Arimathea was one of the seventy disciples Jesus sent out in Luke 10:1; in another, Jewish elders imprison Joseph for attending to the body of Jesus (again, the Jews serve as stereotypical villains) but, anticipating not only the various "jail break" scenes in the Book of Acts (e.g., 5:18-25; 12:6-11; 16:23-39) but also the vanishing of Jesus's body from the tomb, Joseph disappears. Medieval legends connected with the King Arthur story have Joseph taking the holy grail, the cup Jesus gave to his disciples at the Last Supper, to Glastonbury in England (this was very good for the Glastonbury tourist industry).

There is less interest in the fate of Nicodemus, although a few early legends have him continuing to speak on Jesus's behalf and therefore eventually martyred for his proclamation.

I suspect that both Joseph of Arimathea and Nicodemus are historical figures, but what they actually did and said must remain matters of debate. Was Joseph of Arimathea a faithful disciple or not? Did Nicodemus come to believe in Jesus as Lord, or not? We do not have enough historical information to make a definitive decision.

We can read Joseph as one who displays his beliefs not through proclamation but through action. In some cases, especially in places where Christians are a persecuted minority, such action both conveys the Gospel message and preserves the life of the active evangelist. Not all proclamation needs to be done by words.

For Nicodemus, we can read him as enormously respectful of Jesus, but not quite at the point where he is "born from above" or "born anew" by water and spirit (John 3:5). He is the teenager who doubts the supernatural claims of Incarnation and Resurrection but is on board with turning the other cheek and being a sheep not a goat (so Matthew 25). He is the faithful choir member who sings words of praise and finds inspiration in the music but does not believe in what the lyrics themselves proclaim. He is the faithful attendee of the Sunday school class who raises questions of history and of morality but has no interest in theology and Christology. He is even the partner of the faithful Christian, who comes to church, serves on committees, happily sings the hymns, but is not at the point of being baptized or signing the membership roll.

Such individuals (some of whom are reading this book and finding themselves here) are in the pews and sometimes the pulpits. Nicodemus's story does not end with the Gospel of John, and neither does the story of these friends of Jesus. Whether he, or they, will feel that Holy Spirit blow and become born anew cannot be known. Whether it matters is another question that each individual will need to decide.

# Conclusion

# GOD AND NATURE

The Gospels of Mark and Matthew depict Jesus deserted by his friends, taunted by passersby, chief priests and scribes, soldiers, and other victims of crucifixion. In Luke's account, some of the bystanders are not hostile, and some are even sympathizers; Luke also depicts one other victim proclaiming not only Jesus's innocence but also his kingdom and so his kingship. John's Gospel depicts no taunting; instead, Jesus is supported by and supports his mother and his Beloved Disciple, as Mary Magdalene and at least one other woman stands by him. All four Gospels include soldiers at the cross, but only the Synoptics have a centurion express admiration for Jesus. For Matthew and Mark, a centurion pronounces Jesus a son of God. Luke's centurion proclaims Jesus to be "righteous." Each Gospel has a different story to tell.

Such distinctions, which occur throughout the Gospels and not just at this climactic moment, reveal that the story of Jesus's death, like that of his life, was refracted through the different experiences of those whom Luke calls the "eyewitnesses and servants of the word" (Luke 1:2). The story was also developed as Jesus's followers, retelling the events at the cross, understood them through the Scriptures of Israel and, in particular, Psalm 22. Each Gospel writer also had distinct Christological concerns, whether to show how, for persecuted readers, Jesus understood the sufferings of the faithful because he had suffered as well, or, for readers who might have found the weak, humiliated, taunted Jesus intolerable, to show that even in his death he was fully in control.

The list of witnesses the Gospels depict at the cross grows over the centuries. Luke 23:27 tells us that a large number of people, men and women, followed him, and Luke 23:35 records that people were watching. Artists have determined who some of these people were, and the list is marvelously anachronistic. Wealthy patrons arranged to have artists depict themselves and their families kneeling piously—and usually well dressed with designer jewelry—by the cross; other attendees include Saint Jerome, who translated the Bible into Latin; Saint Francis of Assisi; and Catherine of Sienna.

Sometimes present as well, in a symbolic sense, is Adam, who according to Paul allowed sin and so death to enter the world. The apostle explains, "Therefore, just as sin came into the world through one man, and death came through sin, and so death spread to all because all have sinned.... But the free gift is not like the trespass. For if the many died through the one man's trespass, much more surely have the grace of God and the free gift in the grace of the one man, Jesus Christ, abounded for the many" (Romans 5:12, 15). Early commentators noted that Golgotha is Aramaic for "[place of] the skull," and instead of being content with the idea that the location resembled a skull, they asked, "Whose skull?" The answer, which surfaces as early as the Christian writer Origen (184-253), is: the skull of Adam. The blood that drips from Jesus's brow, pierced by the crown of thorns, and the blood that flows from his side, pierced by a soldier's lance according to the Fourth Gospel, flows down to the head of Adam and so redeems him and all humanity.

While art and theology show that anyone can be at the cross, and thus that Jesus, in his dying moments, is never alone, the

Gospels themselves provide two others present at the cross, working together, to assure that despite the despair that Mark and Matthew portray, together with the compassionate promise Jesus makes in Luke's account, and consistent with Fourth Gospel's reigning Christ, lifted up on both throne and cross, everything happens as it should. John's Gospel makes the divine presence clear throughout. In John 10:30, Jesus states, "the Father and I are one"; in 16:32 he repeats, "I am not alone because the Father is with me." The divine presence in the Synoptics is not only anticipated by Jesus's citation of the opening of Psalm 22 (in Mark and Matthew's versions), it is seen by heavenly portents, each with its own symbolic value: the tearing of the Temple veil, the darkness, the earthquake, and the raising of the saints.

## The Tearing of the Veil

Present at the cross in all four Gospels is God, and we see the divine operating through nature and in the material world. According to Mark 15:38 (cf. Matthew 27:51; Luke 23:45), at Jesus's death "the curtain of the temple was torn in two, from top to bottom." The common explanation, heard in numerous sermons, is that the curtain is the one that hung between the (outer) Court of the Gentiles and the Court of the Israelites. The Temple had concentric rings of holiness: for all people, then for all Israel, then Israelite women, Israelite men, priests, and in the center the Holy of Holies, entered by the high priest only on Yom Kippur, the Day of Atonement. Thus, in some conventional preaching, the rending of the veil grants divine presence to the Gentiles, whom the Jews had previously excluded. Sigh. This misreading is what happens when we don't understand Judaism. Jews had always seen God as the God of the world; that they welcomed Gentiles to worship in synagogues and in the Temple as well shows this universalistic part of the tradition. Access to God was always and everywhere possible.

Another popular tradition is that the rending symbolizes the forthcoming destruction of the Temple. While this interpretation is possible, it is not needed, for Jesus had already made a clear statement about the fate of the Temple in Mark 13:2, "Do you see these great buildings? Not one stone will be left here upon another; all will be thrown down." Something more is going on with the veil.

One hint we find in the writings of Josephus, our first-century Jewish historian. Josephus was a priest, and he knew the architecture of the Temple firsthand. In his *Jewish War* 5.212-214, he describes the giant curtain, embroidered by blue, scarlet, and purples, which presented an image of the universe and all that was mystical in the heavens. Thus, the rending of the veil is a symbolic splintering of the universe, much as was that first creation when God said, "Let there be light." Nothing will be the same.

A second hint is that in Jewish tradition, one shows mourning by tearing a piece of clothing. Here, with the rending of the veil, the "house of God," the Temple Jesus called "my Father's house" (Luke 2:49) is mourning at the loss of this precious son. In case this explanation of the divine presence and so divine mourning is not convincing, attention to the Greek may help. Behind the English translation of the term "torn" in Matthew 27:51 // Mark 15:38 // Luke 23:45 is the Greek term from which we get the word "schism." The term appears elsewhere in Mark only in 1:10, when the heavens are "torn" and the Spirit descends on Jesus at his baptism. God is present at the cross, and God is mourning for his son.

## Darkness

The Romans crucify Jesus at the "third hour" which is nine in the morning. Mark 15:33 reports, "When it was noon, darkness came over the whole land until three in the afternoon" (cf. Matthew 27:45; Luke 23:44). There is no such darkness reported in the Fourth Gospel; such darkness would be inappropriate, for it is here, in John 8:12 and elsewhere, that Jesus proclaims, "I am the light of the world. Whoever follows me will never walk in darkness but will have the light of life."

As with the famous star of Bethlehem (which for Matthew's original audience is not a star in the sense of a giant ball of hydrogen gas, but a living being), for which astronomers futilely hunt in the effort to support the claims of a miracle with science (and so ironically downplay the miracle), so, too, with the earthquake and the darkness. Sleuths propose an eclipse (unlikely at Passover, which takes place at the time of the full moon), a dust storm, heavy cloud cover, the ash from a volcano, and whatever else makes scientific sense of the report. This strikes me not only as a futile exercise but a theologically inappropriate one. We do better to spend less time trying to explain an account of a miracle and more time trying to discern what we do with the information the Gospel writers provide.

In the ancient world, heavenly portents at the births and deaths of famous people—emperors, warriors, demigods, even philosophers—were standard fare. For the Synoptics, this darkness can evoke numerous allusions to the Scriptures of Israel, starting with the "darkness that covered the face of the deep" in Genesis 1:2 and so indicated a time of chaos prior to creation. The darkness thus prepares us for the new beginning, a new dawn. Or the darkness reminds us of one the ten plagues, when "Moses stretched out his hand toward heaven, and there was dense darkness in all the land of Egypt for three days" (Exodus 10:22). Yet the plagues, signs of divine power that bests the power of the gods of ancient Egypt, also portend salvation from slavery. For others, darkness is a reminder of the curses expressed at the end of Deuteronomy, which concerns the implications of social breakdown: "You shall grope about at noon as blind people grope in darkness, but you shall be unable to find your way; and you shall be continually abused and robbed, without anyone to help" (Deuteronomy 28:29). The best intertextual match to this description, and one that I think influenced Mark, comes from Amos, speaking of what we have come to call the "Day of Judgment." Amos writes, "On that day, says the Lord God,

> I will make the sun go down at noon,
>     and darken the earth in broad daylight.
> I will turn your feasts into mourning,
>     and all your songs into lamentation;
> I will bring sackcloth on all loins
>     and baldness on every head;
> I will make it like the mourning for an only son,
>     and the end of it like a bitter day.
>
> *Amos 8:9-10*

The image of darkness coupled with the Day of Judgment and especially with a reference to mourning for an only son spoke to the early followers of Jesus.

## The Rocks Split, and Earthquake, and the Raising of the Saints

Matthew adds to the notice of the curtain, "The rocks were split. The tombs also were opened, and many bodies of the saints who had fallen asleep were raised. After his resurrection they came out of the tombs and entered the holy city and appeared to many" (Matthew 27:51-53). In 27:54, Matthew explains that what had happened was an earthquake. It is these portents at the cross, not Jesus's death, that prompts the centurion to confess that Jesus was a "God's Son." Were the Gospels to be judged for special effects, Matthew's scene would be in the running.

The Gospel of Matthew delights in offering what are known as "fulfillment citations," verses that begin with some variant of the formula, "This was done to fulfill what was said by the prophet...." Sometimes the allusions appear without the formula, as is the case for the numerous allusions to Psalms 22 and 69 in the description of Jesus's crucifixion. With these miracles, Matthew is again evoking prophetic texts.

In Jewish tradition, one of the signs of the inbreaking of the messianic age is a general resurrection of the dead, followed by a final judgment. Matthew, however, delays that time in order for the disciples of Jesus to "make disciples of all nations" (Matthew 28:19). To assure readers that the messianic age has begun, not only does Matthew depict the resurrected Jesus greeting the two women and then commissioning the disciples, but Matthew also notes that others were resurrected with him. That general resurrection for Matthew has begun. Should we have additional questions for the Evangelist at this point—what did these raised saints look like? Were any heroes of ancient Israel? Whom did they visit? What happened to them?—we have only our imaginations to provide answers.

Today's culture has a fascination for ghosts and zombies, and in almost all these stories, these revivified bodies are both malevolent and unattractive. I am prompted, by reading Matthew in light of such popular cultural tropes, to wonder how we understand both the idea of resurrection and also our notion of our own bodies. Death is less likely to be feared if we know we will not be alone, that our bodies will be treated with respect, and that our memories will live on.

## And Now?

God was present all along, as was the spirit that Jesus breathed out in John's account. The heavens were opened, God mourned, and nature, too, mourned. More, we know the end of the story. Mourning will turn to joy; joy will turn to commission. Death will come again, and so, the text promises, will come new life.

In the end, we can't with much surety determine who was at the cross, other than the soldiers. In offering different configurations of the people at the cross and different descriptions of what they said and did, the Gospel writers are not attempting to record what happened, as if they are transcribing videotape. They are telling a story about Jesus of Nazareth, his life and his death, and the story they tell is based on how they understand Jesus. With their templates, the story continues.

I see the witnesses at the cross first as figures we all might try on: Do we doubt, or sometimes even scoff? Do we, like those who read the titulus, wish Jesus really were that political rebel who brought about the end of Rome? Do we see ourselves sometimes carrying that cross ourselves, as did Simon of Cyrene? Might we be waiting for a miracle, when nature speaks miracles all around us? Are we waiting for that sign from heaven in order to believe, or are we content to follow our friends who do have this faith because we see how it works for them? Do we admire Jesus but not find ourselves worshipping him as a divine Son, and if so, do we find ourselves welcomed among those who do have such faith? Are we parents whose children confound us or who travel paths we do not want them to take? Who comforts us in their absence? Are we blended families, beholding new parents and new children? Are we citizens, horrified at what is done by our governments or its agents? Do we seek mercy for the crimes we have committed, or do we despair that nothing can be done? For each figure at the cross, we can provide backstories, words to speak at the time, words to speak the next day, and words to speak on "day one," that first Easter Sunday.

When Jesus in the first two Gospels cries out the first line of Psalm 22 and the bystanders think he is calling Elijah, I am reminded of 1 Kings 19:11-15. God tells the prophet, "Go out and stand on the mountain before the LORD." The prophet obeys. "Now there was a great wind, so strong that it was splitting mountains and breaking rocks in pieces before the LORD, but the LORD was not in the wind; and after the wind an earthquake, but the LORD was not in the earthquake; and after the earthquake a fire, but the LORD was not in the fire; and after the fire a sound of sheer silence" (vv. 11-12).

Listen closely. Jesus has died. The witnesses have departed, some to their homes and some to the roads leading out of the city, some back to elegant palaces and others to carry a body to a tomb. Some scoff; others weep and beat their breasts. Two will remain affixed to crosses, unless someone else comes to claim their bodies. The soldiers will take Jesus's garments, and one centurion will wonder at what he had witnessed. God and nature remain, but we all come away from the cross changed in some way.

For witnesses, memories are fragile. They fade with time. They transform when others share the story of the same event. Sometimes as the witnesses tell the story they elaborate, or they use a metaphor that will become for later hearers a fact. Points get lost, or found, in translation. Rather than engage in the futile attempt to determine who exactly these witnesses were, what they saw, and what they did, we readers do well to listen to their stories and see how their stories transform us. At that point, we pick up the story ourselves.